Fast Projects

PEARSON
Prentice Hall
BUSINESS

Books to make you better

Books to make you better. To make you *be* better, *do* better, *feel* better. Whether you want to upgrade your personal skills or change your job, whether you want to improve your managerial style, become a more powerful communicator, or be stimulated and inspired as you work.

Prentice Hall Business is leading the field with a new breed of skills, careers and development books. Books that are a cut above the mainstream – in topic, content and delivery – with an edge and verve that will make you better, with less effort.

Books that are as sharp and as smart as you are.

Prentice Hall Business.
We work harder – so you don't have to.

For more details on products, and to contact us, visit
www.pearsoned.co.uk

Fast Projects
Project management when time is short

Fergus O'Connell

PEARSON
Prentice Hall
BUSINESS

Harlow, England • London • New York • Boston • San Francisco • Toronto • Sydney • Singapore • Hong Kong
Tokyo • Seoul • Taipei • New Delhi • Cape Town • Madrid • Mexico City • Amsterdam • Munich • Paris • Milan

PEARSON EDUCATION LIMITED

Edinburgh Gate
Harlow CM20 2JE
Tel: +44 (0)1279 623623
Fax: +44 (0)1279 431059
Website: www.pearsoned.co.uk

First published in Great Britain in 2007

ISBN: 978-0-273-71233-6

British Library Cataloguing-in-Publication Data
A catalogue record for this book is available from the British Library

10 9 8 7 6 5 4 3 2 1
11 10 09 08 07

Typeset in IowanOldStBT 10/16pt by 30
Printed by Ashford Colour Press Ltd., Gosport

The publisher's policy is to use paper manufactured from sustainable forests.

For Clare

Contents

Acknowledgements

Thanks so much to my editor at Pearson Education, Samantha Jackson. Her energy, creativity and enthusiasm for this book appear on every page of it.

Thanks to Karen Molloy and Val Downey for holding the fort, for all their work and ingenuity, for never giving up, for not panicking (too often) and for their courage over the last five years.

This book is dedicated to Clare, *l'amore della mia vita*, wise, loving and beautiful.

List of figures

About the author

Fergus O'Connell is one of the world's leading authorities on project management and getting things done in the shortest possible time. *The Sunday Business Post* has described him as having 'more strings to his bow than a Stradivarius'. He has a First in Mathematical Physics and has worked in information technology, software development and general management.

Fergus has spent much of the last thirty years either doing, teaching, learning, writing or thinking about project management. In 1992, he founded ETP (www.etpint.com), which is now one of the world's leading programme and project management companies. His project management method – Structured Project Management/The Ten Steps – has influenced a generation of project managers. In 2003 this method was used to plan and execute the Special Olympics World Games 2003, the world's biggest sporting event that year. His radical methods for shortening projects are in use by a growing band of devotees. His experience covers projects around the world; he has taught project management in Europe, North America, South America and the Far East.

Fergus is the author of seven books, both fiction and non-fiction:

- *How To Run Successful Projects – The Silver Bullet*, 3rd edition (2001)
- *How To Run Successful High-Tech Project-Based Organizations* (1999)
- *How To Run Successful Projects In Web-Time* (2000)
- *Simply Brilliant – The Competitive Advantage of Common Sense*, 2nd edition (2004)
- *Call The Swallow* (2002)
- *How To Do A Great Job – And Go Home On Time* (2005)
- *Fast Projects: Project Management When Time Is Short* (2007).

The first of these, sometimes known simply as 'The Silver Bullet', has become both a bestseller and a classic. *Simply Brilliant* – also a bestseller – was runner-up in the W H Smith Book Awards 2002. *Call The Swallow* was shortlisted for the 2002 Kerry Ingredients Irish Fiction Prize and nominated for the Hughes & Hughes/Sunday Independent Novel of the Year. His books have been translated into twelve languages.

Fergus has written on project management for *The Sunday Business Post*, *Computer Weekly* and *The Wall Street Journal*. He has lectured on project management at University College Cork, Trinity College Dublin, Bentley College, Boston University, the Michael Smurfit Graduate School of Business and on television for the National Technological University.

He has two children and lives with his partner in France.

Introduction

Projects that take longer than expected have become pretty much a cliché in the modern world. Hardly a day goes by that we don't read or hear about some project somewhere that has been delayed or missed its deadline – sometimes repeatedly. Governments, companies large and small, organisations in the public and private sectors, individuals – nobody seems immune from this terrible condition.

And what a pity! *Because it doesn't have to be like this.*

- It is possible to run projects that *don't* run over.
- It is possible to get these projects done with the least amount of work – far less than would have been involved had the project run over.
- And it is even possible to deliberately shorten projects.

In short, it is possible to run *fast projects* – projects that don't run over, can often come in early and never require huge amounts of effort to keep them on the straight and narrow.

You don't have to have a title like Project Manager, Project Leader, Team Leader to do this (or to benefit from this book). The book is for anybody working in any industry or sector where they have been handed an undertaking and told to make a success of it. If you want your project to

- come in on time or early
- be done as painlessly as possible

then this book is for you.

Here's how the book is organised. There are twelve chapters. The first eight show you how to plan and execute any project. They take you from the moment the project is handed to you through to doing a post-mortem on a completed project.

These chapters are structured as follows:

- There's a section at the beginning which cuts to the chase and describes, as succinctly as possible, the basic idea of each chapter and exactly what you have to do on your project.
- Then a number of sections follow which give a bit more background to the basic idea. You can read them or not as you wish.
- Each chapter ends with a section that extends the basic idea. The purpose of this extension is to show you how you can significantly shorten your project. If you are trying to get your project done in the shortest possible time then you will need to read this.

Chapters 9 through 12 give you some additional tools to help you deal with projects using the least amount of time possible. Specifically, these tools are:

- How to assess a project in five minutes (Chapter 9).
- How to scope and plan a project in a day. (The technique is described in Chapter 10 and an actual scoping and planning session is described in Chapter 11).
- A checklist of the principal reasons why projects fail (Chapter 12).

The book is quite prescriptive. Rather than saying 'you could try this, or here is a bunch of ways to do that', it attempts to provide as foolproof a recipe as possible. As a result, while there may be a number of ways to do particular things, this book will, in general, say 'do it this way'.

Finally, this book is for people running projects large and small, in work/outside of work, involving a cast of thousands or just one person. The biggest project that the methods in this book have been applied to is the Special Olympics World Games 2003, the world's biggest sporting event that year and widely regarded as an outstandingly successful project.

If you want to build up a track record of outstanding success on projects then this book will take you step by step through doing exactly that.

I'd like to know whether you found the book useful or whether it made any kind of difference. Or not! With that in mind you can e-mail me at fergus.oconnell@etpint.com with any brickbats or bouquets (or anything in between). You can also find more project management resources at www.etpint.com.

CHAPTER 1

SAY 'WE'LL TAKE A LOOK AT IT'

Don't agree to something that's impossible

If you want to run a fast project then the first thing that you definitely *don't* want to do is commit to something – a deadline, a budget, a target – that is completely impossible. The lesson of this first chapter is very simple: don't agree to anything until you've had a chance to look at it.

Projects are dangerous things

Your boss calls you into his office, gathers up the pile of stuff and says, 'Congratulations, you're going to be leading the poison chalice project and I'm sure it'll be a career-enhancing move for all of us. Oh, and by the way, we don't know much about this project, but it has to be done by this date, you'll have to do it with the team you've got and the budget is fixed.'

Project management is one of the hardest jobs in the world. This is because you get asked to make a prediction of the future and then make that prediction come true. Now, if you – or any of us – could actually do that, you wouldn't be here. You certainly wouldn't be reading this book. Instead, you'd be down at the race track or at the casino or buying lottery tickets. But instead you make predictions of the future for a living and try to make those predictions come true.

"You make predictions of the future for a living and try to make those predictions come true"

If all of that wasn't bad enough, you also get asked to make these predictions in a very strange way. Imagine your car was acting up and you took it to the garage and you said to the mechanic, 'I don't know what's wrong with my car, but I'd like you to fix it in the next half hour and it better only cost fifty euros/pounds/dollars.'

You can't really imagine such a dialogue happening. Yet, in a lot of sectors and industries and organisations, such conversations are routine. Somebody says, 'Here's the project. We don't know much about it, but it's got to be done by this date, for this budget, with these resources.' And often everyone just says, 'OK.'

The project 'missile'

The handing over of the project, as described above, is a dangerous moment. It's such a dangerous moment that it's like having a missile fired at you. There are two types of missile – the ballistic missile and the cruise missile. The ballistic missile is launched and you pick it up on your radar screen. The ballistic missile is the explicit handing over of the project as described in the opening paragraph.

But there is also the cruise missile – the sneaky one. It gets launched somewhere and suddenly, out of nowhere, it seems, it lands in your lap. Here's an example of a cruise missile. You're at a meeting, say, and somebody asks you, 'How long do you think that would take?' If you're not careful, you'll think up an answer. And if you're not really, *really* careful, you could end up opening your mouth and making a commitment.

Whether the missile is ballistic or cruise, it's dangerous because it carries a warhead. But in our line of business – project management – the missile carries a particularly dangerous kind of warhead called the *binary warhead*. A binary warhead contains two things which separately are pretty innocent but mix them together and they're deadly.

"The missile carries a particularly dangerous kind of warhead called the *binary warhead*"

In our case, these two things are:

- The request itself – 'will you do the poison-chalice project?' is an example of a request.
- Something that is often referred to as the 'constraints' or – my own preferred term – 'the baggage'.

The baggage is the idea that even though they've asked you the question, 'How long will that take?', they already know the answer:

- The project must be finished by a certain date   Date baggage
  And/or
- It must be done for a certain budget   Budget baggage
  And/or
- It must be done with certain resourcing   Resource baggage.

'Defusing' the warhead

If you try to deal with the request and the constraints together, I hope you can see that potentially you could end up in a lot of trouble. Because as you think about the date, you think about all the things you'll have to do and all the time that those things will consume. Meanwhile the baggage is telling you that you're not going to get the time.

And you're thinking that you're going to need three highly skilled specialists for a certain part of your project. The baggage is telling you that you'll be lucky to get a man and a dog!

And, in almost every case, the baggage has a tendency to win the argument. As a result you can end up committing to doing things that are

- difficult to do
- impossible to do
- well beyond impossible (if such a place exists).

It has to be said that the number one reason why projects fail is that they were never actually possible in the first place. Somebody said, 'Here's the project. It has to be done by this date or for this budget' and everybody just said, 'OK.'

"The number one reason why projects fail is that they were never actually possible in the first place"

So if you're going to run your projects successfully, the first thing you have to do is to stop this behaviour. From now on, when a project is handed to you, you're not going to just say, 'OK.' Instead you're going to do what the mechanic or the plumber or the doctor or the truck driver or the assistant in the clothes shop or any one of a million other 'normal' professions does when asked to address a problem. They say, 'We'll take a look at it.' In other words they'll do an examination, come up with a diagnosis and then tell you what's possible and what's not.

In all likelihood, the powers-that-be may be looking for *action* to break out straight away. Once you walk out of your boss's office, he may want to see meetings and brainstorming sessions and teleconferences and documents being written and people doing stuff and all the other paraphernalia of a live project.

It doesn't matter.

All you can say at this stage is, 'We'll take a look at it.' All you commit to is that you're going to look at the problem and see what's possible and what's not. And with that you walk out carrying the pile of stuff and turn your attention to Chapter 2.

"All you commit to is that you're going to look at the problem"

'We'll take a look at it'

Whether it's a large, cast-of-thousands project or a seemingly modest request, the rule is always the same – don't agree until you've had a chance to look at it. OK, there may be things that you've done many times before and you know precisely how long they will take and how much work is involved, but for anything else, get the time to examine it and understand it.

The method for examining it and understanding it is described in Chapters 2–7. Once you've read through these chapters and you understand what you have to do, you will find the following.

For small things, you'll be able to figure them out (almost literally) on the back of an envelope; for large things you will have to write a detailed plan. Using the techniques described, I think you will be pleasantly surprised at how much of a plan you can build in a short space of time. On our courses we generally give people 2–3 hours and in that time they end up building plans for large and complex projects. In building these plans they uncover so many things about the project. These are things which, if they hadn't been uncovered, would have turned into surprises and so-called 'firefighting' further down the line.

The payback for the time spent doing this early planning is huge. The payback is all the time you save by *not* having to firefight things. I think you'll agree that it wouldn't take much of a firefight to blow away 2–3 hours of your time.

So:

You're at a meeting and somebody is pushing for 'a date'. Ask for a time-out – ten minutes, half an hour, a couple of hours, depending on the scale of the project – so that you can come up with a reasoned answer to their question.

Somebody comes running in saying that they need an answer by four o'clock today as to whether something can be done or not. Insist on the time you need to apply Chapters 2–7 and do your analysis of the project.

Somebody says, 'This is a very small thing – could I just get you to do it now?' Don't be suckered. How many 'very small things' have you seen turn into very big things?

Somebody says, 'We don't have time to plan – just go do it.' Your response should always be, 'We'll take a look at it.'

If you took away only one idea from this book, let it be this idea: if you stopped reading now, provided this was what you did then you would have picked up something really, really useful.

CHAPTER 2

FIGURING OUT THE GOAL OF YOUR PROJECT

How to figure out the goal of your project

If you want to have a fast project, the key thing is to know precisely what you're being asked to do. In order to do that, do the following:

1 Ask yourself the question, 'What event marks the end of this project?'

2 Make a list of all the project stakeholders and for each stakeholder write down their win-conditions. A stakeholder is any individual or group of people affected either positively or negatively by your project. Win-conditions are the things that would make a successful project for that stakeholder.

3 The point in time you chose as the end point of your project should deliver all of the win-conditions. If not, the point in time needs to change or else some of the win-conditions need to change.

"Win-conditions are the things that would make a successful project for that stakeholder"

Using the material generated from doing this, you can then, for example, fill out project charter documents, project initiation documents or other similar documents used by your organisation to launch projects.

Example of figuring out the goal of a project

Let's say your project is to 'run a job advertisement'.

What event marks the end of this project?

Well maybe it's when the advertisement runs in the paper, but maybe you wouldn't really regard that as a successful ending to this project. Maybe it's really about whether you get fifty resumés or application forms in response to the advertisement? Or maybe it's not about the number of resumés but the quality – do you get five good ones? Or maybe it's about whether the advertisement gets you somebody you can hire? Or is it about whether that person turns out to be any good, so that the event that marks the end of the project is actually the successful completion of their six-month probationary assessment?

I hope it's clear that I'm not saying that one of these endings is right and all the others are wrong. All of them are possible valid endings. What's important, though, is that all the stakeholders are agreed on the ending that has been chosen.

Make a list

Make a list of all the stakeholders and their win-conditions. Here it is.

Stakeholder	Win-conditions
Us	• Run ad that reflects well on the company and doesn't upset anybody. It also should communicate why the jobs on offer are so attractive that you'd be mad not to apply
Our boss	• The ad sends out a positive message about the company
Existing employees	• Doesn't upset anybody – uses only material that is in the public domain • Sends out a message that the company is one that people want to work for
Potential employees	• Sends out a message that the company is one that people want to work for
Our customers	• Sends out a message that the company is expanding and is a good company to do business with

A point in time

Now you can pick any point in time which will deliver these win-conditions.

Bounding the goal

The first thing you need to do after you've been handed the project is to put a boundary around the project and say that these things – within the boundary – are part of this project and those things – outside the boundary – are not. Think of a box. Everything within the box is part of the project, everything outside the box isn't. For those things within the box you should also decide – in conjunction with the stakeholders – what is have-to-have and what is nice-to-have.

If you fail to fix this boundary, then you can think of a cloud. The problem with projects whose goals are cloud-like is that they can't finish. (I think you'll agree that this is a pretty serious problem indeed!) They can't finish because what lies within the project boundary isn't defined. What will happen then is that the team will want to deliver as little as possible, the rest of the stakeholders will expect as much as possible and the resulting gulf in expectations will be the cause of great human unhappiness. This is up there with the big project killers and is probably the number two reason why projects fail or get into trouble.

"The problem with projects whose goals are cloud-like is that they can't finish"

My stakeholders don't know what they want

They say that they'll know it when they see it. So I'm not going to be able to bound the goal of my project.

No problem. It's fair enough if they don't know what they want. Then this is what you do.

You say that you will work with them to go through a number of iterations to come up with the goal. You will make an initial shot at it. You will assume whatever you have to assume to enable the goal to be bounded. You will then deliver that goal. They will check it out, see whether they like it or not. If they do, you're done. If they don't, then you can come up with a revised goal and deliver that.

Keep doing this until they get what they want. Just be sure to remind them – because they will be more than happy to forget – that each of these iterations will take time and effort.

Controlling changes to the goal

Assume you succeed in bounding the goal and then you start the project. What happens then? Well, what happens then is that changes start happening. Something you should have thought of but didn't; something the stakeholders never mentioned or that you misunderstood; a change in the business or regulatory or political climate; changes in staffing or resourcing levels, and so on. These changes are an inescapable fact of life on the project and there's no problem with them provided you *control these changes*, i.e. you have some form of change control.

So here's the next big mistake that project managers make. They make the mistake of thinking that because they have committed to a plan and a schedule and a budget for the project, the stakeholders can change their minds any way they want and the plan, the schedule, the budget must still hold.

"The stakeholders can change their minds any way they want"

Now this is clearly nonsense, as the following simple example shows. Suppose the project is to make 'a container for water' and you believe that what you've been asked to make is a glass. Now it turns out that that was not really what the stakeholders wanted. They really wanted a jug – a container for water, sure – but with a spout and a handle. Or a swimming pool – that's also a container for water.

Now the plan, the budget, the schedule for a swimming pool is clearly not the plan/budget/schedule for a glass, but many project managers make the mistake of thinking that because they've made commitments, these commitments must hold in all circumstances. As the example shows, this is ridiculous.

The customer is always right

So why do project managers do this? How could they be so stupid? Well, of course, project managers aren't stupid and they make these decisions with the best of intentions and for the most noble of reasons. And that reason is the old saying, 'The customer is always right.'

Yes, the customer *is* always right. Absolutely. The customer can change his mind any way he wants. He is completely within his rights to do that. But then you as the project manager are within your rights to say, 'OK, but here's what the effect of that will be.' Then the customer can decide whether he wants to go ahead with the change or not.

Here's a different way of looking at change control that is perhaps more gut-level. When a change occurs on a project – be it a big change like we don't want a glass, we want a swimming pool – or a little change – Charlie's gone sick for half a day – there are only three ways you can respond to that change.

The first is to declare it to be a significant change. A significant change occurs on a project when the basis upon which the plan was built is altered. 'We don't want a glass, we want a swimming pool' is an example of a significant change; Charlie's gone sick for half a day is not.

> **A significant change occurs on a project when the basis upon which the plan was built is altered**

The second way you can respond to a change is that if you have contingency in your plan – this is discussed in Chapter 5 – you can use the contingency to cover the change.

But

- if something isn't a significant change
- or it is, but you refuse to call it such
- or you don't have contingency in the plan, either because you didn't put it in
- or you did, but then some genius took it out (and you didn't stop them)

then the only other choice open to you is to work harder – longer hours, come in at weekends, take work home, cancel personal things.

My stakeholders keep changing their minds

That's OK. They're within their rights to do that. But every time they change their minds, you're within your rights to tell them what the effect of that change will be – in terms of extra time needed and/or resources required and/or additional budget.

Notice, too, that you're actually not within your rights to say 'OK' to them every time they ask for something new/different.

There is always a price associated with every change of mind.

Making sure you pick the right goal

Finally, you want to make sure that you pick the right goal. And the right goal is the one that makes as many of the stakeholders happy as possible.

This book is all about running successful projects, so maybe it should have started out by defining what a successful project is. If it had done that it would probably have ended up saying things like, 'on time', 'within the budget', 'meeting the requirements' and so on. All good stuff. But if you want it in a nutshell, a successful project is all about happy stakeholders. They start out happy – in the sense that they know what they can realistically expect from the project – and they end up happy in that that is what they get.

A good way of describing this is to say that you must 'maximise the win-conditions of the stakeholders'.

Each stakeholder in a project has win-conditions. Win-conditions are 'here's what would make a successful project for me'. In general different stakeholders have different win-conditions. Often win-conditions are diametrically opposed. Also, different stakeholders' win-conditions can have different levels of importance.

❝Different stakeholders' win-conditions can have different levels of importance❞

So what you need to do is to

- identify all of the stakeholders
- understand all of their win-conditions
- then see if you can come up with a composite set of win-conditions that all of the stakeholders can live with.

This is what maximising the win-conditions of the stakeholders means.

I hope it's clear that if you miss out on certain stakeholders, or you fail to identify particular win-conditions, the chances of you delivering them by accident are fairly remote. Then you will have stakeholders whose win-conditions haven't been met, i.e. you will have met stakeholders' *lose-conditions*, i.e. you will have unhappy stakeholders, i.e. you will have an unsuccessful project.

Shortening your project

Even for very large projects it's possible to get this whole business of fixing the goal done very quickly. Chapter 10 describes a method for fixing the goal of a project in less than a day. (The chapter actually describes a method for scoping and planning a project, i.e. carrying out everything that's in Chapters 1–7, in one day.)

CHAPTER 3

FIGURING OUT WHAT WORK HAS TO BE DONE

Projects get done because a whole bunch of jobs get done. At some point somebody, i.e. you, the project manager, has to figure out what those jobs are and sequence them. If you want to have a fast project then the best time to figure out the jobs and do the sequencing is at the beginning of the project. Detail is the key to getting the list of jobs as accurate as possible. If you want to shorten your project, then an increased level of detail is the key to doing that.

Get the right people

Involve the people who will do the project (the team) in figuring out the list of jobs. If they're not available, maybe a subset of the team is. If that's not an option, get somebody to help you. The worst thing you can do is to do this by yourself.

Identify the big pieces of work

Identify the big pieces of work to be done in the project, the bits that get you from the start to the end. There's no need to be too accurate at this point. Broad brush strokes are fine. It may be that your organisation has a standard lifecycle that it follows for projects. If that's the case, follow that. Just ask yourself what are the big lumps of work that have to be done to get you from the start to the end. Note, too, that there are going to have to be chunks of work that ensure that each stakeholder's win-condition gets met. Win-conditions don't just get met by accident!

&&Win-conditions don't just get met by accident!&&

Identify all the little jobs

Within each of these big pieces of work, identify the detailed jobs that have to be done. Break everything down such that each job you identify is between 1–5 days' duration or 1–5 person-days of work. (If you're confused about the difference between duration and work, it's explained later in this chapter.) Be as specific and concrete as possible, i.e. rather than saying 'requirements gathering' say 'Charlie meets with the IT people for two days to explain his requirements'.

Where you don't know something, make an assumption

The big problem in estimating a project is that you don't have all the facts, all the knowledge. Assumptions are powerful because you make up facts. If you come to a piece of the project and you say, 'I haven't a clue about this', then just make up something. You don't know how much testing there is going to be in your project because you don't know how many errors you're going to find when you come to test it? No problem, just make an assumption – assume three rounds of testing or thirty-three or whatever. If you have some information from previous projects to guide you, that's great. Otherwise just make up something that seems reasonable. You will see instances of assumptions in the example which follows.

Build a work breakdown structure (WBS)

Store all the little jobs that you identify in a Work Breakdown Structure or WBS, i.e. show the project as being made up of the big pieces of work, which in turn are made up of the smaller pieces.

The parameters of a job

Notice that what you're doing when you estimate is trying to come up with all of what might be called the *parameters* of a job. These are things like:

- the job itself
- what other jobs it depends on
- how much work is involved in that job
- how long that job will take (its duration)
- how much the job will cost (its budget)
- who will do it
- how much these people are available
- when they will do it.

It's a lot of stuff to try to estimate all at once. For this reason, I find it better at this stage to just focus on *some* of these things. I would suggest that at this stage you focus on the first four, i.e.:

- the job itself
- what other jobs it depends on
- how much work is involved in that job
- how long that job will take (its duration).

The problem in estimating

Project management is about predicting the future. The trouble is that none of us can do it with 100% accuracy – and yet your stakeholders expect your predictions to be 100% accurate.

❝Project management is about predicting the future❞

There is an exercise we do on our training courses where we describe a hypothetical project to the audience and then ask them to estimate a single task of this project. The task is to review a particular document on the project. We give the audience as much information as we can and answer any questions they have. The smallest estimate we've ever had for this exercise is half an hour; the largest is six months! The exercise shows that estimating accurately is very difficult. But it is not impossible, provided you follow the method described above.

Estimating properly

There are two things you can do to help you. One is to record what happened on previous projects – how long particular tasks took, how much work was involved in them, what they cost – and use this information when you come to plan your next project. (How to do this is described in Chapter 8.)

However, whether you have comparable information from previous projects or not, the key to getting the prediction as right as possible is *detail*. By breaking down the work to be done into small elements of detail, you are less likely to miss vital elements of the project. That is what the method described above does.

Making the method work

In making the method work it is important for you to realise that you are building a sequence of events. This has the following implications:

- Each event in the sequence has to be crystal clear, i.e. it has to say exactly what is going on in that event. 'Charlie reviews the spec for half a day with the two marketing people' is crystal clear. 'Module F', for example, isn't.
- There has to be cause and effect between the events, i.e. each event must lead to the next event.
- The events must be chained together.

So how do you do it? What are the key questions you have to ask? It's very simple. They're questions like:

- 'So what's the first thing that happens?'
- 'Who does what?'
- 'And what happens then?'
- 'And then?'

If you ask these questions you'll always be able to build the sequence of events as accurately as possible.

Duration and work

The difference between these two quantities is something which (a) often causes major confusion and (b) introduces errors in estimates. Here is the difference between duration and work.

- **Duration**, sometimes also called elapsed time, is *how long* a particular job is going to take. It is measured in the normal units of time – hours, days, months and so on. The duration of a soccer match, for example, is ninety minutes.

- **Work**, sometimes called effort, is how much work is in a particular job. It is measured in units like man-days, person-hours, person-years and so on. The work in a soccer match, counting two teams of eleven, a referee, two assistant referees and a fourth official, is twenty-six times ninety minutes i.e. thirty-nine person-hours.

❝Work, sometimes called effort, is how much work is in a particular job❞

Durations are important because they enable you to figure out *how long* all or part of a project will take. If you figure out all of the individual task durations, string all of the tasks together, showing what can overlap and what can't, then you will end up with the total duration of your project.

But if you want to know what size a project is or what a project will cost, duration won't tell you. Instead you need to know how much work is going to go into each task. Then if you know the cost of this work (for example, using daily rates), you can figure out what the project is going to cost, i.e. its budget.

The project management job

As project manager you must make sure that all of the jobs identified in your Work Breakdown Structure get done. As with any of these jobs, the project management job must also be estimated. Here's a rule for doing that.

From the WBS take the total work – not the duration – in the project. Take 10% of this. This will be sufficient to cover the project management. Insert a job into the list of jobs called 'Project Management'. Its work will be the number you have just calculated. Its duration will be the duration of the project.

What you have to do if you're the project manager

If I really wanted to bore you senseless I could suggest to you that we talk about 'the roles and responsibilities of the project manager'. Hmm! What an exciting thought – to come up with some kind of checklist or job description so that the next time you run a project you know what to do.

Yes, we could do it – we could give you a list of roles and responsibilities. But in my view, that's not half as helpful as giving you a role model – somebody you should behave like if you're tasked with running a project.

I don't know what kind of movies you like and whether you like westerns. If you do – or even if you don't – you may be familiar with a type of western which is the cattle drive movie. I'm sure you know how they go. We start out on the Rio Grande with five thousand head of longhorns (cattle) and our job is to get them to Abilene or Kansas City or some such place. The project manager's job then is to 'trailboss' the herd of jobs to the conclusion of the cattle drive.

So this is what you must do if you're the project manager: you must do anything necessary to ensure that each and every job gets done. You must take responsibility for *all* of the jobs in the WBS. In general, the set of jobs breaks down into two – those being done by 'our people' and those being done by the others, i.e. people in other departments, organisations, companies. Despite the fact that you may have no obvious leverage over these people, e.g. they don't report to you, it is still your job to make sure that these jobs get done.

❝You must take responsibility for *all* of the jobs in the WBS❞

You must also give priority to project management tasks. Many people, in their projects, have both project management work to do and actual jobs on the project. The project management jobs must always take precedence.

Example of the 10% calculation

Suppose the total work in your project is 400 person-days and the duration of the project is 4 months. Then 10% of 400 is 40 person-days. This is how much project management this project will require. The 40 person-days will be spread out over the life of the project, i.e. over the 4 months and so, on average, this project will require 10 person-days a month project management. Assuming there are about 20 days in a month, running this project is going to be a half-time job (10 days every 20) for the project manager.

Example of using this method to build a WBS

The section of WBS in Figure 3.1 was built using the method just described. The big pieces of work are those numbered 1.2 and 1.3 – Project planning and scoping meeting and Produce Requirements Document. The tasks underneath those are all the little jobs. Either as a result of the names of the jobs and/or the notes in the 'Notes' column, every job is very 'specific and concrete'. So, too, is the sequence of events that has been built.

		Task Name	Work	Predecessors	Notes
1		1 The Project	36 days		
2		1.1 START	0 days		
3		1.2 Project planning and scoping meeting	9 days	2	9 people for 1 day
4		1.3 Produce Requirements Document	27 days	3	
5		1.3.1 Research user requirements	7 days		
6		1.3.1.1 Gather info on competitive products	0.50 days		Charlie'l do it
7		1.3.1.2 Review with marketing	2 days	6	Assume 3 marketing people and Charlie @ 1/2 day each gives 2 days Work. It's a half day meeting where
8		1.3.1.3 Identify users	0.50 days	7	Marketing guy - his estimate
9		1.3.1.4 Prepare user questionnaires	2 days	8	Charlie says he'll do it. Take him a couple days.
10		1.3.1.5 Distribute questionnaires	0.50 days	9	An Admin. person. Estimate is on the basis that 1/2 day is the smallest unit we recognise.
11		1.3.1.6 Retrieve questionnaires	0.50 days	10FS+1 wk	Half a day's work chasing. Probably 5 days elapsed time to get it done
12		1.3.1.7 Analyse information	1 day	11	Charlie and a Marketing person @ 1/2 day each
13		1.3.2 Write requirements document	9 days	12	Charlie. Use company standard 9 section format @ 1 day pers section
14		1.3.3 Review cycle	18.50 days	13	
15		1.3.3.1 Circulate	0.50 days		Admin person - basis for estimate is same as for 'Distribute questionnaires' above
16		1.3.3.2 Individual review	2.50 days	15	5 reviewers, half day each, allow 1 week elapsed time in which it has to happen
17		1.3.3.3 Review meeting	3 days	16	Charlie and 5 reviewers @ 1/2 day each
18		1.3.3.4 Changes to document	2.50 days	17	Charlie - his estimate
19		1.3.3.5 Circulate again	0.50 days	18	Same as earlier 'Circulate'
20		1.3.3.6 Second review	1.50 days	19	5 reviewers, 1-2 hours each, try and do it ASAP - so give reviewers a deadline to respond with comments.
21		1.3.4 Signoff	0.50 days	14	Assume there will be no substantial changes. Admin person chases signoffs.
22		1.3.5 Requirements complete	0 days	21	

Figure 3.1 Section of Work Breakdown Structure (WBS)

27

Project management tools

If you're involved in project management then sooner or later the subject of a project management tool will come up. Which one to choose, which is the best, should you pick Microsoft Project or a free one off the Internet, or do you need an enterprise-wide project management tool?

Relax! People built the Pyramids without paper. The Allies won World War I without a computer.

To do anything you need two things – a recipe (or method) and a set of tools. This book is about a recipe. Once you know the recipe, you know how to cook the dish. Then you can find a tool or set of tools that will help to make your life easier when you're cooking.

In terms of choosing a tool, my advice would be to use the simplest tool that gets the job done. So, if you can put the plan on a piece of flipchart paper or a whiteboard, do it. Moving up from that you can write the plan in a document on a computer. This is useful because invariably the plan will need updating and having it on a computer is good for that. Moving up from that again you could put the plan into a spreadsheet. Or you can get yourself Microsoft Project or a Microsoft Project-type tool if you feel that will help.

All of these tools, whether you pay for them or not, have strengths and weaknesses. This is true of even the big, expensive, enterprise-wide tools. For example, MS Project does some things wonderfully well (e.g. enabling the building of the Work Breakdown Structure) and is woeful at other things (e.g. I'm not convinced it calculates the critical path – the shortest time in which the project can be done – correctly).

I think the only way you can choose a tool is to try it out. Get one or two people to use the tool on real projects, find out where it's strong and whether you can live with its weaknesses. If you feel that you can endure the weaknesses, then use the tool. Otherwise move on and try another one.

In general, I would say move to a more complex tool only if you find that the limitations of the simpler one are causing you a problem. You could also use a combination of tools.

Numerous assumptions appear in the 'Notes' column. The four parameters of a job, mentioned above, are also shown, namely:

- the job itself
- what other jobs it depends on – this is shown by the column headed 'Predecessors'
- how much work is involved in that job
- how long that job will take (its duration) – shown in the bars on the right-hand side.

Finally, if the piece of WBS shown was the entire project – it isn't – then its project management requirement would be 3.6 person-days (10% of 36 person-days) and its duration would be from early January to early March (the duration of the project).

How to estimate absolutely anything

It's possible to estimate anything – even things you know very little about. Here's an example.

"It's possible to estimate anything – even things you know very little about"

I'm assuming that very few of the people reading this were around at the time of the Normandy landings on D-Day. I'm also assuming that very few readers have a military background which would make them qualified to plan this project.

However, let's see how you would have done if you had been handed this project. Here's a plan for a little piece of it.

First, identify the big pieces of work. Here's a possible breakdown:

1 Start.

2 Get soldiers.

3 Ship them to just off the Normandy coast.

4 Have them get ashore.

5 Get past defences to objectives for first day.

6 The end.

Now (arbitrarily) take item 4 and break it down further:

4.1 Put soldiers in landing craft.

4.2 Run landing craft into shore.

4.3 Open bow door.

4.4 Soldiers wade through surf and reach dry land.

And then here's your sequence of events:

Task	Dependency	How much work?	How long?
4.1 Put soldiers in landing craft	Item 3	Assuming 30 soldiers in a landing craft and each one takes 2 minutes to board, then 1 person-hour	Assume 3 board simultaneously – note that will need 3 rope ladders per landing craft to do this, then 20 minutes
4.2 Run landing craft into shore	4.1	Assume the distance is 2 miles and knowing the speed of the landing craft is 5 miles per hour, then 24 minutes for 30 people = 12 man-hours	24 minutes
4.3 Open bow door	4.2	30 people for 1 minute = $\frac{1}{2}$ man-hour	1 minute
4.4 Soldiers wade through surf and reach dry land	4.4	Assuming this is being done under heavy enemy fire, that the distance is 200 yards and people do it as quickly as possible, how long to wade through 200 yards of shallow surf? Do experiment to find out. In the meantime, assume 6 minutes. 6 minutes for 30 people = 3 man-hours.	6 minutes
TOTALS		$16\frac{1}{2}$ man-hours	51 minutes

Now, some day I hope a military person will read this and will maybe correct all the flaws in it. In the meantime I think you haven't done badly at all. The 'How much work?' column is probably not particularly relevant in a project like this. I presume people weren't too concerned with the *financial* aspect. But notice the things you found out.

The issue of how many ladders there are per landing craft is very important. This will determine how quickly the landing craft can be filled. So, too, is the speed at which heavily laden men can wade through surf. An experiment on this will provide vital information, i.e. there's something you should/can do early in your project to provide you with valuable information. (Many projects have similar issues where if you schedule the project such that you do some work early, you can find out valuable knowledge which can then be used to replace your assumptions.) Finally, knowing whether the duration of this piece of the project is fifty-one minutes or not is crucial in terms of determining when to launch the landing craft. This will be tied to sunrise time, daylight calculations and tides.

You may argue that I picked an easy one – that I should have picked 5: 'Get past defences to objectives for first day'. So, OK, pick that one:

5.1 Get past defences on the shoreline and the beach.

5.2 Get past defences at the back of the beach.

5.3 Get off the beach to that day's objectives.

Now, take one of these – arbitrarily the first one – and come up with the sequence of events. (This time omit the calculations of man-hours.)

Presumably somebody also did calculations about how many soldiers might be needed to cross the beach given that a proportion of them would be killed or wounded in trying to do so. Maybe military people have rules of thumb for things like this. In their absence we could do these calculations by making assumptions.

Task	Dependency	How long?
5.1 Get past defences on the shoreline and the beach	4.4	Assume that the only defences on the shoreline and beach are 'hedgehogs' – cross pieces of girders welded together. These plus machine gun shooting from the back of the beach. Will have to do aerial reconnaissance to confirm what obstacles are there. If the obstacles are mined, will have to get the mines cleared before the soldiers go ashore. If can't find out, should assume that they are mined. If the concrete machine gun emplacements haven't been destroyed by the earlier bombardment, won't be able to do anything about them. Beach is (say) 200 yards wide at this point. Do experiments to see how long for a heavily loaded soldier to cross 200 yards of sandy beach. In the absence of this, say 5 minutes. Plus allow several blocks of time for being pinned down – say 3 blocks of 5 minutes each. Total 20 minutes to get to the back of the beach.

There you go – that's how you estimate properly. If you can do it for this project, wouldn't you agree that you could do it for any project?

Shortening your project

To shorten your project there is a small but crucial change that you make to the method described at the beginning of the chapter. Instead of breaking things down so that each job you identify is between 1–5 days' duration or 1–5 person-days of work, you *break them down such that each job is either one day's duration or one day's effort*. By doing this you ensure that every day on your project is accounted for and – ultimately – will be spent wisely. (This is what film-makers do, for example, when they build what's called a 'shooting schedule' – the project plan for shooting a movie.)

> **"You ensure that every day on your project is accounted for and – ultimately – will be spent wisely "**

Obviously there is an overhead involved in doing this. But this will be repaid many times over by the shortening that will occur on your project as a result of doing it. Figure 3.2 shows a piece of Work Breakdown Structure but this time broken down to the one-day level of detail. It is represented on a spreadsheet.

Why the one-day level of detail?

The answer to this question can be found by looking at the reasons why projects take more rather than less time.

As I write this, I've just come from a little project to run a recruitment advertisement in the newspaper. This project has taken much longer than any of us intended and the reasons why are very instructive because this project exhibited most, if not all, of the things that cause projects to take more rather than less time. These things were as follows:

Column headers (diagonal): Charlie · Engineer #2 · Engineer #3 · Engineer #4 · Technical author · Marketing people (3) · Admin Assistant · Reqs. Reviewers (5) · Test & Design Reviewers (2) · Tester #1 · Tester #2 · Users · Project Management

1	09-Jan-07	3 Proj 3 Project planning and scoping m 3 Project planning and scoping meeting ... 3 Project planning and scopir
2	10-Jan-07	6 Gathe
3	11-Jan-07	9 Prepare user questionnaires
4	12-Jan-07	9 Prepare user questionnaires ... 10 Distribute user questionnaires
5	15-Jan-07	
6	16-Jan-07	7 Review with Marketing ... 7 Review with Marketing
7	17-Jan-07	
8	18-Jan-07	
9	19-Jan-07	11 Retrieve questionnaires
10	22-Jan-07	12 Analyse information
11	23-Jan-07	13 Write requirements document
12	24-Jan-07	13 Write requirements document
13	25-Jan-07	13 Write requirements document
14	26-Jan-07	13 Write requirements document
15	29-Jan-07	13 Write requirements document
16	30-Jan-07	13 Write requirements document
17	31-Jan-07	13 Write requirements document
18	01-Feb-07	13 Write requirements document
19	02-Feb-07	13 Write requirements document
20	05-Feb-07	15 Circulate document
21	06-Feb-07	
22	07-Feb-07	
23	08-Feb-07	
24	09-Feb-07	16 Individual review [1/2 day each]
25	12-Feb-07	17,18,19 Review meeting / changes to document (inc. circula 17 Review meeting [1/2 day]
26	13-Feb-07	17,18,19 Review meeting / changes to document (inc. circulate again)
27	14-Feb-07	17,18,19 Review meeting / changes to document (inc. circulate again)
28	15-Feb-07	20-22 Second review/ Signoff / Reqs complete [1/4 18-20 S 18-20 Second review/ Signoff / Reqs complete [1/4 day]

Figure 3.2 Work Breakdown Structure with one-day level of detail

1 The goal of the project wasn't clear. Sure, we were running a recruitment ad, but current and potential customers would also see it. If we wanted it to, it could also say things to them. Once we realised this, it took us extra time we hadn't planned on to build in these other facets. In general, this can be described as the goal of the project not being properly defined, so that new things to be done are constantly coming to light or being identified. There were other stakeholders with win-conditions that we hadn't taken into account. Once we realised this there were extra things that had to happen to factor in these other stakeholders.

2 The process by which the ad would be written and approved wasn't really worked through. In the end, many more people than we had originally imagined had input to the review and signoff. In other

words, many more jobs than we had originally expected needed to be done.

3 This business of the process is important. I once heard it said that projects were a bit like adultery – periods of frenzied activity interspersed with periods of just waiting around. This effect was certainly experienced on our project where a bout of furious activity was followed by a lull in the fighting while we waited for the next step to be carried out.

4 No one person was responsible for getting the ad done.

5 Nor was it 100% explicit who would be needed at what times to provide text for the ad or to review the results. In other words, not only was the process not clear but the responsibilities at each stage of the process were not clear either. (And, of course, if the process wasn't understood, how *could* the responsibilities be identified?)

6 A corollary of this was that since people didn't know they would be needed, they had arranged to do other things and so were unavailable when their time came. (It should be noted, too, that often, even when people *do* know they will be needed, they have inadvertently or otherwise overbooked themselves and so are unavailable.)

7 Nobody had planned this little project and in particular nobody had identified what the critical path was. (The critical path is the shortest time in which the project can be done.) As a result, nobody was really focused on the effect a delay in one piece of the project might have on the rest of it.

8 A corollary of this is that nobody knew what, if any, advantages there might be to completing their bit of the project as quickly as possible.

9 A second corollary was that, in general, people being people would leave their bit to as late as possible before starting. (Not knowing the critical path, this seems an innocent enough activity.)

10 Maybe it's a separate thing, maybe it's an accumulation of all of the preceding things, but I call it 'Where did the week go?' syndrome. Did you ever have one of those weeks when you get to the end of it and you wonder where the days could have disappeared to and what the hell you achieved? No? Lucky you!

As a result of these things, the ad drifted on and days were lost waiting for people to fit things into their schedule and come back with their piece done, so that the next bit could take place. It's important to say, too, that none of the things that had to get done was a surprise – once we thought about it. *The problem was we didn't think about it.*

The things that we have identified above are common to projects in all industries. But there are some industries that are far better at dealing with them than others. The film industry is one where, with some well-publicised exceptions, the problem of projects overshooting the schedule and the budget has largely been solved. *The Lord of the Rings* trilogy, for example, was a colossal, $300 million project. Yet its three releases came in on time and within budget, meeting the three release dates.

How does the film industry do this? The answer is that it builds a very detailed plan of how the movie will be shot. The plan is called a shooting schedule. A shooting schedule is a day-by-day, person-by-person plan of how the project will be carried out. Where most plans in our kinds of projects are pious hopes about the future – 'wouldn't it be great if it turned out like this?' – shooting schedules are anything but pious hopes. Shooting schedules are *descriptions* of the future – 'here's how we intend things to go' – and by and large movie people will try to ensure that things do go that way.

Now you may argue that there is a difference between making a movie and the kinds of projects that we tend to be involved in. I will argue that there are far more similarities than differences. And these days most movies are project managed with an accuracy which would make the most pernickety accountant happy.

"Most movies are project managed with an accuracy which would make the most pernickety accountant happy"

Conventional wisdom says that for projects in knowledge and high-tech industries it is not possible to build a day-by-day, person-by-person plan. My answer to that is 'Nuts!' It's possible. I know because I've done it. Figure 3.2 is a fragment of exactly such a plan. And if you build a one-day level of detail plan, what will happen? Well, the answer is that all of the above causes of project overshoots will pretty much disappear because:

1 The goal of the project will be well defined – otherwise you would not have been able to build such a plan.

2 All the jobs needed will be in your plan.

3 There will be no delays because your plan will give you the precise sequencing of the jobs.

4 Managing the project will be very straightforward because you will know what everybody has to do every day.

5 Your plan will show you exactly who is needed at what time.

6 Since people will know when they are needed, they will ensure their availability well in advance.

7 You will see exactly what a delay is going to do to the project.

8 You will be able to see exactly what the effect of starting a task early is going to be.

9 You will be able to see exactly what the effect of finishing a task early is going to be.

10 You will know exactly what has to be done in any given week of the project.

'That's all very well,' I hear you say, 'but on knowledge and high-tech projects things change – sometimes radically.' Or, 'We're in the blah sector and it's completely volatile and things will constantly be changing over the life of the project.'

Yes, yes – of course things will change. But we already know how to deal with changes. We have our three possible responses, given in Chapter 2, namely:

- significant change
- use the contingency
- work more hours.

CHAPTER 4

GETTING PEOPLE TO DO THE WORK

Like many things in life, project management is a problem in supply and demand. The demand comes from the work to be done. (This was identified in Chapter 3.) The supply comes from the people to do the work. In theory your job is very simple. If there are 100 person-days of work to be done, there had better be 100 person-days of people to do the work.

If you want to have a fast project you want to make sure that this supply–demand equation stays in balance – that there's always enough supply to match demand. Unfortunately the demand has a tendency to go up as stakeholders ask for more things, extra things, 'Can it do this?', 'I thought it was going to do that'. If that isn't bad enough the supply has a tendency to go down as you never seem to have enough resources to do all the work. Every time the two go out of balance, this will cause 'drag' on your fast project, causing it to slow down. Most of your project management life will be about trying to bring these two quantities into balance. If they go out of balance for too long then the whole project can crash and burn.

> **"Most of your project management life will be about trying to bring these two quantities into balance"**

To be completely precise, one should really say 'resources' here rather than people. However, since in most projects it's the people resources which are the problem, this is what you focus on.

There are three issues here:

- people being there to do the work.
- those people's availability.
- the strengths and weaknesses of those people.

By factoring in these things, you add in to your plan the other 'parameters' discussed earlier in Chapter 3, i.e.:

- who will do the job.
- those people's availability.
- when they will do the job.

You could also – if you chose to – determine

- how much the job will cost (its budget)

simply by knowing the cost of the work that you have identified in Chapter 3.

The three people-related issues – people, availability and strengths – are discussed in the following sections.

People

You need people to do the work. It's quite common that at the beginning of a project, you don't know who some or all of those people are. Then it is customary to indicate these on the plan with so-called 'generic resources'. These are names like 'A N Other', 'New hire', 'Contractor #3', 'Java Programmer' and so on. No problem with this, except that before the job starts, there has to be a *real* person in place to replace the generic resource.

All so obvious, you might say, it's ludicrous to even be writing it. However, an enormous number of projects go wrong due to the fact that not all the jobs got done because there weren't people doing them.

Your first job, then, is to track down the people who are going to do the work. For real people you stick them in the plan and that's the end of it. For generic resources, you put them in together with tasks in the plan to do some legwork necessary to find/hire/recruit/get those people.

People's availability

Imagine Charlie shows up one day on your project. He's been sent by central casting and announces that he's to be your financial specialist. Great. Your first task is to ask Charlie whether he's available full time. Sure, he nods enthusiastically. This is a project he really wants to work on. He's got no other project on the go at the moment. Great. Oh, there is the Project Y wind-down that's going on, but that's just gonna be 1 or 2 days for the next week or two. OK. 'And I've gotta go to a meeting with a customer that marketing's arranged,' adds Charlie brightly. Oh-kay. 'I've booked some holidays,' says Charlie, somewhat more uncertainly. You ask when and he tells you. Enough already. You need to find out Charlie's *real* availability. A dance card, which is described next, will enable you to do that.

Dance cards

The term 'dance card' is a reference to those more genteel days – I don't remember them myself! – where, when ladies went to dances, they were issued with dance cards. A dance card was a list of tunes that the band was going to play. To dance with a certain lady, you wrote your name in a certain slot on her dance card. Then that dance was taken, that slot was booked and could not be given to anyone else. Understanding people's real availability is about understanding the 'bookings' they already have.

66Understanding people's real availability is about understanding the 'bookings' they already have99

So you do Charlie's dance card with him and it ends up looking something like in Figure 4.1.

It shows that over the next six weeks, when the financial work on your project was intended to be lifting off, Charlie has no time at all available to work for you. In a period of thirty working days, Charlie has forty-two days' work to do – even before he begins to include your project. Also – to put it mildly – he looks like having a few heavy weeks. Charlie looks at it in stunned silence. You lift the phone and call central casting.

#	Project	Basis		01/11	08/11	15/11	22/11	29/11	06/12	Total
1	Project Y wind-down	2	dpw	2	2	2	2			8
2	Meeting with customer	1	day	1						1
3	PLC Conference	3	days			3				3
4	Support of Project X	0.5	dpw	0.5	0.5	0.5	0.5	0.5	0.5	3
5	Reviews of other designs	4	days	1	1	0.5	0.5	0.5	0.5	4
6	Admin. / Inbox / Interruptions	1.5	hpd	1	1	1	1	1	1	6
7	Training others	1.5	hpd	1	1	1	1	1	1	6
9	Support of Project Z	1	dpw	1	1	1	1	1	1	6
10	Holidays	5	days					5		5
	Available	30	days							
				7.5	6.5	9	11	4	4	42
	Notes:									
	(1) 'dpw' = days per week									
	(2) All figures in person-days									

Figure 4.1 Charlie's dance card

Now obviously I made Figure 4.1 come out a certain way to make a specific point. In my experience, however, getting people to do dance cards is almost always a sobering experience. For you it is an invaluable tool to enable you to establish the real availability of individual people for your project.

If you find on one of your projects, any of the following symptoms

- jobs are not getting done
- people working longer and longer hours
- projects falling further and further behind

then a possible cause of this is that you're not getting the effort that was originally budgeted for in the plan. A dance card check would be a good way to establish this.

Strengths and weaknesses

People are good at some things and not good at others. To assume that people are 'plug and play' – just drop them into a slot and they'll work out – would be very foolish indeed. I'd like to think that not a lot of people would consciously make such a mistake. But I think many people do it unconsciously. Or perhaps, phrased a different way, they neglect to think about the issue at all.

"People are good at some things and not good at others"

The point is, though, that you *have* to. How you use or misuse the talents (and weaknesses) of your team will have everything to do with the outcome of your project. There are lots of ways one could approach this. A way I've used for a long time that I find works well is to rate the assignment of people to jobs according to the following scheme:

1 The person has the necessary skill and experience to do the job and likes/loves to do it (Superstar).

2 The person has pretty much all the skills and experience to do the job and is prepared/happy enough to do it (Solid citizen).

3 The person has the necessary skill and experience to do the job but doesn't have enough time available. (A dance card check would establish this.)

4 The person can be trained or instructed in doing the job.

5 The person cannot do the job (Loose cannon).

While the project manager can do this, an even better way is to have both the project manager do it and each individual team member do it for the jobs to which they have been assigned. Then compare the results. They are always interesting. Misconceptions you may have had about a particular person, or that they may have had about themselves, inevitably surface and may well result in some reassignments.

Example of adding people and their availability

This example (Figure 4.2) takes the section of Work Breakdown Structure from the previous chapter and adds

● who will do the work

● those people's availability.

You begin by putting in the names – either people's names where they're known or generic resources where they're not – against jobs. Your notes and assumptions (shown in the 'Notes' field) assist you here.

	Task Name	Work	Predecessors	Resource Names	Duration
1	1 The Project	46 days			238.50 days
2	1.1 START	0 days			1 day
3	1.2 Project planning and scoping meeting	3 days	2		1 day
4	1.3 Produce Requirements Document	37 days	3		236.50 days
5	1.3.1 Research user requirements	7 days			19.50 days
6	1.3.1.1 Gather info on competitive products	0.50 days		Charlie	0.50 days
7	1.3.1.2 Review with marketing	2 days	6	Analyst #1 20	5 days
8	1.3.1.3 Identify users	0.50 days	7	Marketing guy	0.50 days
9	1.3.1.4 Prepare user questionnaires	2 days	8	Charlie	2 days
10	1.3.1.5 Distribute questionnaires	0.50 days	9	Administrative	0.50 days
11	1.3.1.6 Retrieve questionnaires	0.50 days	10FS+1 w	Administrative	5 days
12	1.3.1.7 Analyse information	1 day	11	Analysts	1 day
13	1.3.2 Write requirements document	9 days	12	Charlie	9 days
14	1.3.3 Review cycle	20.50 days	13		207.50 days
15	1.3.3.1 Circulate	0.50 days		Administrative	0.50 days
16	1.3.3.2 Individual review	2.50 days	15	Requirements	5 days
17	1.3.3.3 Review meeting	3 days	16		0.50 days
18	1.3.3.4 Changes to document	12.50 days	17	Charlie	12.50 days
19	1.3.3.5 Circulate again	0.50 days	18	Administrative	0.50 days
20	1.3.3.6 Second review	.50 days	19		0.50 days
21	1.3.4 Signoff	0.50 days	20	Administrative	0.50 days
22	1.3.5 Requirements complete	0 days	21		0 days

Figure 4.2 Section of work breakdown structure with people assigned

The availability is indicated by the percentage number shown on the right-hand side. For example, 'Administrative Assistant (10%)' means that the Administrative Assistant is available 10% of her time, i.e. half a day per week; 'Requirements Reviewer (50%)' means that someone is available half-time.

Shortening your project

You'll remember from the previous chapter that if you wanted to shorten your project, you had to break it down to the 1-day level of detail. You'll remember, too, how the plan was represented (Figure 3.2). Here, the who's-going-to-do-the-job has already been factored in – as has their availability. While representing the project like this may have seemed like a lot of work at the time, I hope you can now see that, in the long run, you save yourself time because your entire plan gets built at once.

CHAPTER 5

MAKING THE PLAN BULLETPROOF

Unexpected things will happen on your project. Most of those unexpected things will be *bad*, i.e. they will have a negative effect on the project and tend to blow it off course or slow it down. If you want to have a fast project, you want to try as far as possible to reduce the effect of these things.

You have to realise that the plan as it stands is a very fragile thing. If you were to go with this plan, then as soon as the first little whoopsie happened on the project – Charlie goes sick for half a day, for example – you start to fall behind schedule and bang goes your fast project. So you must take your fragile, delicate plan and toughen it up. You want to make it robust so that you can send it out into the world and it can survive a few knocks. You will do this using two related techniques – contingency and risk analysis.

Contingency

You don't want to make commitments to your stakeholders based on best possible case. Instead, given that you know that bad things will happen on your project, make some allowance for them and *then* make your commitments. They're far more likely to come true.

If you don't put contingency in your plan – or you put it in but then you allow someone to take it out – you lose one of the three responses to change that were discussed in Chapter 2. The result is that any change which occurs on your project either has to be a significant change or you will have to do additional work to deal with it. Many of the things which happen on projects could not be classed as significant changes – somebody goes sick, something is delayed, something takes longer than expected and so on – and so for all of these types of events, you (and your team) will have to work extra.

"Many of the things which happen on projects could not be classed as significant changes"

This is hardly a smart idea.

Risk analysis

Risk analysis says, wouldn't it be nice if you could figure out where the hot spots on your project are likely to be – those places where you know you're going to have difficulty. Worst case, you'll be aware of them. However, maybe then you cannot just be aware of them but you can actually do something about them. Maybe you can reduce the likelihood that they will happen, or reduce the effect if they do happen, or eliminate them altogether. 'If you don't actively attack the risks on your project,' the saying goes, 'then the risks will actively attack you.' Let's do it to them, then, before they do it to us.

Putting contingency in the plan

There are all sorts of ways that contingency can be put in plans. Here are some of them:

- You can divide what the project is delivering into have-to-haves and nice-to-haves. You deliver the have-to-haves and deliver the nice-to-haves if you have time. If you deliver only the have-to-haves, you get a faster project. If you deliver the have-to-haves and you run out of time, then you jettison the nice-to-haves.

- You can add an additional, say, 10–15% onto the total work. This will be your contingency.

- If you feel people (generally, your management or stakeholders other than your team) will want to take out your contingency, then you can hide it so that they _can_ find it. You could do this, for example, by increasing the work amount assigned to each job.

can't

- There is an argument to be made for putting contingency in explicitly _and_ hiding it. The stakeholders get the satisfaction of taking it out; you still have it in there and if you stop them from taking it out you have twice as much. If you do this, you won't get any arguments from me since the more contingency you have in the plan, the greater the likelihood that the commitments you make to stakeholders will come true.

"There is an argument to be made for putting contingency in explicitly _and_ hiding it"

- For my money, though, the single best way to do it is to add some extra time onto the end date. It has loads of advantages. It is very visual, very easy to track against, very simple to spot drift and hugely effective as an early-warning system.

The next chapter discusses how to sell the contingency to the stakeholders, in particular to the team and to the powers that be.

Doing a risk analysis

A simple and very effective way to do a risk analysis is to go through the following steps:

1 Identify – in a brainstorming session – the risks to the project. Risks are the things that can cause the project to get into trouble.

2 For each risk, grade it in terms of the likelihood of it happening. Use a three-point scale: 3 = high, 2 = medium, 1 = low.

3 For each risk, grade it in terms of, if it were to happen, what would its effect be? Use the same three-point scale.

4 Multiplying (2) by (3) gives you your exposure to that particular risk – the larger the number, the greater the risk.

5 For each risk, identify what action(s) you can take to reduce that risk.

6 For each risk identify how you will know whether that risk is actually starting to happen.

These are sometimes called 'early transition indicators'.

The result of this will almost certainly be some additional jobs that must then be put back into the plan – in the list of jobs – and processed from there, i.e. effort estimated, dependencies established, people identified to do them. This will in turn affect the project management effort calculation.

Risk analysis example

In a brainstorming session with (a) just your team or (b) some of the stakeholders or (c) all of the stakeholders, ask them to start proposing risks. To kick-start the proceedings you might have a list in one of your back pockets of the ten most common reasons why projects fail. Here it is.

Ten most common reasons why projects fail

1 The goal of the project isn't defined properly.

2 The goal of the project is defined properly, but then changes to it aren't controlled.

3 The project isn't planned properly.

4 The project isn't led properly.

5 The project is planned properly but then it isn't resourced as was planned.

6 The project is planned such that it has no contingency.

7 The expectations of project participants aren't managed.

8 The project is planned properly but then progress against the plan is not monitored and controlled properly.

9 Project reporting is inadequate or non-existent.

10 When projects get in to trouble, people believe the problem can be solved by some simple action, e.g. work harder, extend the deadline, add more resources.

Say your group eventually comes up with eight risks. (Again, this is intended to be illustrative, rather than exhaustive.) They are listed and graded in Figure 5.1. They are as follows:

1 The team you are inheriting are borderline burnout cases. In your view this is a major issue and your exposure is very high here.

2 So-called 'scope creep', where the scope of the project changes as a result of a series of uncontrolled changes. For example, Marketing ask for 'just one more feature' and Product Development agree to slip

it in. Or, more dangerously, Marketing people creep down to Product Development and ask individual engineers. Or, more dangerously still, some engineer suddenly thinks 'this would be really neat'.

3 You're deeply offended when they suggest the next one – poor project management! You let them grade its likelihood at 2.

4 You don't get enough supply to match the demand. This is your big fear.

5 This is another of your big fears – people leave. Maybe it's already covered to some extent by number 1, but you want it highlighted.

6 And this is your third big one. It all falls apart if Charlie, your key man, leaves. You're reasonably close to Charlie and don't think he's job hunting at the moment. But you never can tell.

Risk	Likelihood	Impact	Exposure = L x I	Action(s)	Early transition indicators
1 The latent burnout kicks in	3	3	9		
2 Scope creep	1	3	3		
3 Poor or inadequate project management	2	3	6		
4 Inadequate resources	3	3	9		
5 People leave	3	3	9		
6 Charlie leaves	2	3	6		
7 Estimates are wrong	2	3	6		
8 Project is technically infeasible	1	3	3		

Figure 5.1 Risks with corresponding exposure

7 Estimates are wrong – always a fear. You don't grade it 3 because you believe that the approach you used to build the WBS and work estimates is sound.

8 The project turns out to be technically infeasible. Low risk – you're not really blazing a technical trail here. The sophistication is in the set of features you've packaged together, not the technology or software architecture you're using.

Next you add in the risk reduction actions (in Figure 5.2).

1 You're going to try to make this project a happy one. You want to run this project without endless amounts of continuous overtime. You've read Tom DeMarco's book *The Deadline*[1] and it's confirmed what you've suspected for a long time – that continuous overtime doesn't give extra productivity. It isn't even neutral on productivity. *It actually reduces it.*

2 You reckon you can keep a lid on this one.

3 'It won't happen,' you say, looking them in the eye while your stomach churns. They watch, unimpressed, while you write it down.

4 You write it down again. This time you're the one who stares intimidatingly at them.

5 You suggest that HR open up a recruitment pipeline, so that there are at least some resumés from likely candidates in the hopper. It's not much but it's something. Maybe also some incentives for the team.

6 The incentives will be the key here.

7 You need to be on the lookout for the first sign of drift between what was estimated and what actually starts happening.

8 In the unlikely event that this did happen, maybe you would have to start again.

Risk	Likelihood	Impact	Exposure = L x I	Action(s)	Early transition indicators
1 The latent burnout kicks in	3	3	9	• Avoid long hours	• People leave • Morale plummets • Project starts to run late
2 Scope creep	1	3	3	• Project manager stops it from happening	• Project starts to run late
3 Poor or inadequate project management	2	3	6	• It won't happen	• Project starts to run late
4 Inadequate resources	3	3	9	• It won't happen	• Project starts to run late
5 People leave	3	3	9	• HR to get in some resumés • Possible incentives	• People leave
6 Charlie leaves	2	3	6	• Possible incentives	• Charlie leaves
7 Estimates are wrong	2	3	6	• Monitor estimated against actuals to ensure early warning	• Project starts to run late
8 Project is technically infeasible	1	3	3		• Design and/or code phases take longer than estimated

Figure 5.2 Risks with risk-reduction activities

Shortening your project

There's nothing additional you need to do here.

CHAPTER 6

SELLING THE PLAN

Now that you've got your plan, the next thing to do to ensure that your project runs as quickly as possible is to talk the stakeholders through the plan. This way, they will be very clear (a) what they can expect and (b) what is expected of them. I think of this as 'selling' the plan.

In my experience, this is one of the areas that project managers in general are not good at. It's what could loosely be termed 'communications'. More precisely, it's about keeping the stakeholders involved at all stages with regard to how the project is unrolling. It's about managing the stakeholders' expectations. Since we've defined a successful project to be happy stakeholders, there could hardly be a more critical area of your project.

This activity, important on conventional projects, is crucial on fast projects. It's crucial because days lost due to misunderstandings, or people being confused about something, or people being grumpy about something, days lost for whatever reason, can never be recovered. The more you can ensure that this doesn't happen by keeping everyone in tune, the better your chances will be of having a fast project.

Project kick-off meeting

The place to do all of this is at a meeting to kick off the project. There are two constituencies that need to be addressed: (a) the team and (b) the powers-that-be, i.e. your management, customer and any other external stakeholders. It's perfectly feasible to have them both at the one meeting. Sometimes, however, especially on large projects, there is a lot of detail that the team needs to know that the other stakeholders don't. If you felt that was the case for you, then it would probably be better to have two separate meetings.

For both sets of stakeholders the purpose of the meeting is the same – to explain the big picture and everybody's part in it.

"The purpose of the meeting is to explain the big picture and everybody's part in it"

Whether you have one meeting or two, they can both adopt the following structure.

Get the relevant people together

Get them to bring their diaries/calendars. Issue everybody with a copy of the plan.

Take them through the high-level picture

Talk them through the overall picture – what's being delivered, when it's being delivered, the effort or budget involved, how quality is being ensured, who the team members are, the key assumptions upon which the plan is based and any outstanding issues which have yet to be resolved.

Take them through the detail

Now, take them through the plan job by job, line by line. Ask them to note in their diaries when events that are of particular significance to them occur or when they have to carry out certain jobs. The meeting will almost certainly also generate changes to the plan. Since the stake-holders – particularly the team – have been involved in building the plan, these should be only minor at this stage.

Show them the contingency

Next, show them where the contingency is in the plan. Explain to them what its purpose is (and what it is not!). For instance, supposing:

- Your project starts on 2 January
- Has an end date of 31 August that includes three weeks' contingency.

Then you need to stress to the team that the only end date that exists for them is 10 August i.e. 31 August less three weeks. That is the date at which they must be finished. If that turns out to be the case, great – everybody can go to the beach for the next three weeks! If not, then some or all of the next three weeks can be used to save the team's bacon. But the end date is 10 August, not 31 August.

For the powers-that-be stakeholders, however, the end date is 31 August. *It may be possible* to bring the project in before that date, but today the only date that you're prepared to commit to is 31 August.

Show them the risk analysis

Take them through the risk analysis. If they can add more risks at this stage, so much the better.

"If they can add more risks at this stage, so much the better"

Deal with questions/resolve issues

Answer questions as you go and if some questions throw up issues, do your best to resolve them while the group is all together. (There may be some issues that are of interest only to a smaller group of people and these can be taken offline provided there is a commitment to come back to you with an answer by a certain time.)

CHAPTER 7

WHAT TO DO IF THE PROJECT IS IMPOSSIBLE

If your plan shows that the baggage identified in Chapter 1 is achievable then you're ready to proceed to the execution phase of your project (Chapter 8) and you can skip this chapter.

If that is not the case, i.e. the plan says that the baggage is not achievable, then basically you've been handed an impossible project. You need to consider your next move very carefully. If you agree to do the project, not only will you not have a fast project, but there's every likelihood that you'll have a failed one. This chapter is about avoiding that eventuality.

What to do with an impossible project

The realistic plan that you built – the one that enabled you to diagnose whether or not the project was impossible – is also your tool for dealing with the impossible project.

As stated already, that plan involves four very important variables or parameters. These are:

- What (the project is delivering).
- When (the project is delivering it).
- Work – the amount of work or effort and other resources involved in getting the project done. (Notice that this, in turn, gives us the budget of the project.)

- Quality – there is a whole bunch of jobs or tasks in the plan whose purpose is to ensure the quality of the finished product. (Typically, these are things like reviews, testing, quality assurance, walk-throughs, signoffs and so on.)

When you have an impossible project, you have a version of the plan that the stakeholders don't find acceptable. By varying the four parameters you can come up with other versions of the plan that the stakeholders may like. Here's how you can vary the four parameters.

Reduce what's being delivered

You can 'de-scope' the project, i.e. you can do less. If you have categorised what the project is delivering into 'have to haves' and 'nice to haves', then maybe you just deliver the 'have to haves'. Maybe you can reconsider what you actually regard as 'have to have', i.e. do the categorisation again.

Query the baggage date

Understand the significance of the baggage date you've been given. Some dates are inherently suspect and while probing them doesn't always help, it certainly can't hurt.

- 24 December (or really any date in the approximate range 20 December – 3 January or so, i.e. the Christmas period). I accept that for some projects, e.g. the changeover to the euro, the 31 December date had huge significance. But for many projects these end-of-year dates are nothing more than the yearning of some tidy-minded person somewhere wanting the project to be over. (I accept also that this may be somewhat different in the US where Christmas holidays are generally not so long.)

- Check what day of the week the baggage date falls on. If it's a Saturday or a Sunday, then once again it may not have any real significance. It often means that nobody has actually thought out why the end date is important. When you force them to do that it may buy you some extra time. (Once again, I accept that weekend dates can have a huge significance, e.g. they can be to do with taking live systems down and replacing or upgrading them. It's still worth asking, though.)

- In some countries, some months are holiday months, e.g. August in France or July in Sweden, so often – again, not always – a baggage date occurring in these months may not be a real date, or there may be some 'give' in it.

- Finally, the baggage date may be to do with your stakeholders wanting to carve out some contingency for themselves. For instance, they need the thing done by, say, 31 August, but they've told you 10 August. Thus, if you slip, they'll still have a good chance of being on time. So, in this example, 31 August may actually be the real baggage date.

Add more people

You can see what the effect of adding more people to the project will be. You need to be a bit careful with this one because of an effect known as Brooks' Law,[2] which says, 'Adding people to a late project makes it later'.

You can see the truth of this if you think of all the things involved in bringing new people onto a project. There is finding them, recruiting or assigning them, bringing them on board, bringing them up to speed, the time this takes away from existing team members. When you factor all this in, it's easy to see how adding people to a project could have

- little effect
- no effect
- a negative effect.

Nevertheless, it may be possible to parachute in specialists who will be able to hit the ground running. In that case, you may indeed be able to shorten the project, for instance, and perhaps bring a plan date closer to a baggage date.

"It may be possible to parachute in specialists who will be able to hit the ground running"

Use the quality parameter

Finally, it may be that you can reduce the amount of testing or quality assurance (QA) you had planned to do and still have something that the stakeholders will be happy with. Or – more promising – can you get reviews and signoffs done quicker? Can people – especially stakeholders – turn things around quicker, get you decisions faster, so that you can gain some precious days and make the plan date and the baggage date converge? If the stakeholders are pushing you, push some of the responsibility back on to them and show that they, too, can make a contribution to the success of the project and to giving them what they want.

Dealing with reasonable stakeholders

By varying some or all of these four parameters, as just described, you can come up with alternative versions of the plan and you should be able to convince the stakeholders that their best chance lies with one of these. Equally you should be able to discourage stakeholders from choosing a course of action which your plan says cannot be achieved and is doomed to failure.

This is your first, most important and most promising strategy. It should be possible to solve all baggage-type problems in this way. If people are of good will and want the best for the project, this is how these situations should always be handled. Stakeholders asking for impossible courses of action should be told politely but firmly that what they are asking for is not a runner. 'This dog won't hunt!' The plan and the facts in it – and only these – should be used as the basis for any discussion, negotiation and agreement. Anyone engaging in bullying, unreasonable behaviour or trying to pretend there isn't a problem ['So, we're all agreed then – the date's achievable?'] should be pulled back gently to the plan and told to consider the facts.

What if that doesn't work?

If the approach just described doesn't work then you need stronger medicine. You will know if things are not working out because you will end up dealing with situations or with stakeholders where reason no longer prevails. You may hear things like

- 'Saying no is not an option', or
- 'I'm sorry – we just have to do it', or
- 'Sure, it's an aggressive schedule, but I'm sure you'll find a way', or
- 'The problem with you is that you're far too negative', or
- 'You're going to have to learn to be more flexible', or
- 'That's not the culture around here', or
- 'We need can-do people here', or

- 'Don't bring me problems, bring me solutions', or
- 'Is this plan based on a five-day week?', or
- 'If you don't do it I'll find somebody who will', or
- Far worse things.

Sometimes – it has to be said – this pressure to take on an impossible project may not come from external sources at all. You may generate it yourself. You may want to show that you are made of the right stuff, that you have what it takes.

Whether the pressure comes internally or externally, the next sections contain more desperate measures, particularly if you are dealing with unreasonable stakeholders or stakeholders who are behaving irrationally. The aim of all of these measures is to give you a wise decision.

You could say 'yes'

In certain circumstances saying 'yes' may be a wise decision. This may sound like I'm contradicting my previous advice, but I'm not. There's a difference between saying 'yes' on a one-off basis and doing it always. You could possibly choose this tactic if the gap between what the plan says is possible and what the baggage says is necessary is not too great. Suppose you did cancel holidays, work weekends and late nights. If you factored all that additional effort into the plan, would that make things come right? (Notice again that you're using the plan to guide you.)

> **In certain circumstances saying 'yes' may be a wise decision**

If the answer is no, then you need to look at one of the other three tactics which follow.

However, if the answer is yes, you then need to go and say to your team, 'What about it team?' If they're not up for this, you need to move on to one of the tactics which follow. If they are, maybe you want to go back and say 'yes' to your stakeholders.

But if this is truly a once-off, it may be that in these very specific circumstances:

- very definitely a once-off project, and
- gap between plan and baggage bridgeable according to the plan, and
- team up for it

saying 'yes' may constitute a wise decision. However, you are playing with fire. You are taking a drug which can be very hard to get off after you've tasted it once.

You could say 'no'

It may be that everyone has completely lost the plot, i.e. that the gap between what the plan says is possible and what the baggage says is necessary is so great that it could never be bridged.

In that case, you want to get a million miles away from the project because when the bomb goes off here, the mess is going to be appalling. You want to document your reasons for passing on the project. You can add to your document your prediction of what you believe is going to happen (based on the plan), i.e. the mess that is going to be created if this plan is committed to in its current form. Finally, if you really want to rub it in, you can use your plan to say here's how that mess will have to be sorted out when the time comes. All of this should give your stakeholders major cause for thought. In my experience, it has often – though not always – been enough to bring stakeholders around to your point of view.

For you, in these circumstances, saying 'no' might constitute a wise decision.

You could play the change control game

In construction, where the lowest bidder often gets the job, they do this all the time – and highly successfully. (Maybe you know some owners of construction companies who are poor. I have to say I don't know any.)

Let's say that your plan says that the project is going to cost €500K and the stakeholders say you have to do it for €350K. An impossible mission.

You say, 'Sure, I'll take it for three fifty.'

Now, every time the stakeholders make the teeny weeniest change to what they asked for, you slap them with a significant change notice. In addition, you use slips on the stakeholder side to mask any slips on your side.

66You use slips on the stakeholder side to mask any slips on your side99

It could well be that by using this tactic, you take an impossible project and manage your way to making it possible. A wise decision? It could hardly be wiser. People in construction make big profits using this technique.

You could accept the project but not accept the baggage

A neat trick. Here's how it works. Let's say you have a project where the baggage date is 6 September but the plan says 29 November. An impossible mission.

Now, it's important to realise that you have one weakness in all of this – a weakness upon which the stakeholders may pounce. 'Ah ha,' they may say, 'your plan is a prediction and so it could be all wrong. You could have overestimated everything and this project could be very do-able.'

'It could be,' you agree reasonably. 'I could have underestimated everything too, of course, so that the situation could be far worse than I've said here. But here's what I'm prepared to do. I'll give it a try and here's what I guarantee. I don't believe 6 September is possible so I can't guarantee that. I *can* guarantee 29 November. But what I'll also do for you is that every week I'll tell you how we're doing.'

The stakeholders will always accept this – what they heard was you accepting this particular impossible mission. What they believe you said was that you would give the project a try – or, in other words, you're going to have a crack at 6 September.

Now, this is not what you said. So you need to start reminding them. The first week of the project you issue a status report that says:

Here's what you asked for:	6 September
Here's what we're committed to:	29 November
Here's what our plan is saying today:	29 November (Say. It'd be a pretty bad plan if you could not keep it on target for the first week!)

You continue to do this every week. During this time your stakeholders will go through a period of denial where they're not listening to what you're saying. So as well as writing the status report, you need to be bending their ear – we're probably talking primarily about your boss here – and saying, 'What are *you* going to do about this 6 September/ 29 November problem?' The 'you' is a very important word here. This is their problem – not yours. You never committed to 6 September. They did.

You keep doing this until they hear you. Then they may go into a period of irrational behaviour where they start repeating a lot of the things listed at the top of the *What if that doesn't work?* section. However, you're just beaming out the same message:

Here's what you asked for:	6 September
Here's what we're committed to:	29 November
Here's what our plan is saying today:	We'd like to think it would be on or before 29 November!

Finally, if you just stick to your guns and keep beaming out the status reports, they will eventually pass into the third phase where they wake up and smell the coffee and start to deal with *their* (not your) 6 September/29 November issue.

It's worth saying yet again that this tactic prolongs a negotiation that really should have been resolved by varying the four parameters and presenting options. But needs must. This tactic will give you a wise decision – especially if you have one/a group of extremely volatile, disagreeable, maybe even disturbed stakeholders. It should be said, too, that it may not win you friends, but then nobody ever said that being a project manager was a popularity contest.

"Nobody ever said that being a project manager was a popularity contest"

CHAPTER 8

EXECUTING THE PLAN

There are three things you need to do when running the project. The first is to manage people properly; the second is to track progress against the plan; the third is to tell the result of this to the stakeholders. To have a fast project you want to do all of these as quickly and efficiently as possible. This chapter shows you how.

Managing people

You may remember the classification scheme from Chapter 4. It said that when you assigned somebody to a job, one of the following five situations could arise:

1 The person has the necessary skill and experience to do the job and likes/loves to do it (Superstar.)

2 The person has pretty much all the skills and experience to do the job and is prepared/happy enough to do it (Solid citizen.)

3 The person has the necessary skill and experience to do the job but doesn't have enough time available. (A dance card check would establish this.)

4 The person can be trained or instructed to do the job.

5 The person cannot do the job (Loose cannon.)

Using this scheme you can choose where to put in your project management effort over the life of the project.

1 Superstar

Leave them alone and let them get on with it. Even if your natural style is to micro-manage everything, that isn't going to work in this situation. It'll only upset them – plus it will be a complete waste of your time.

2 Solid citizen

If this was a superstar situation then for a five-day job you'd just check on day five and find that the job was done. With a solid citizen you wouldn't be quite so blasé. Here you might check on day 2 and you'd be looking for *evidence* (very important!) that they were making some progress – that some of the deliverables were starting to appear or take shape. You would also want to see that they had a little plan for how they were going to spend the rest of their time. If you were happy about both these things – progress so far and a little plan for the rest – you could consider maybe a little less monitoring more along the lines of the superstar. If, however, you didn't feel a great deal of comfort with either progress or the way forward, you might want to increase the amount of sticking your nose in.

❝You could consider maybe a little less monitoring more along the lines of the superstar❞

4 Trainee

In this situation you'll be all over these people. It will involve training – formal or on-the-job, handholding, helping them to make decisions, correcting them when they go wrong, nurturing them and passing on the benefit of your knowledge. A hands-off style here would basically mean that you're going to throw them in at the deep end and see whether they sink or swim. In my opinion, that would be completely the wrong thing to do. If you start to get some traction with them, you can always then start to move to a more solid citizen-type style.

3 No availability and 5 Loose cannon

You can deal with these two situations together. This in itself is disturbing. No-availability situations often involve solid citizens or superstars, yet their lack of time availability makes them no different than if they were the most wildly incompetent people on the planet.

Here you have two problems. How am I going to get this job done and what am I going to do about this person? To get the job done, you have to find some supply to match the demand. Given that you're always operating in a supply-starved environment, this is going to involve lots of project management effort on your part. Once you get that sorted out, there's the question of what you do about this person. Maybe they had only one job to do on your project and now that's been sorted out there isn't an issue. More likely, though, they have other things to do. If you're in these situations on these other jobs, then you have more fundamental questions about this person. Do you carry them for the duration of the project? Do you fire them or try to foist them off onto somebody else's project? Whatever you choose to do is going to involve large amounts of management effort.

In summary, following an approach something like this means that you put your project management effort in where it will make a difference. You also leave things alone where sticking your nose in would be counter-productive and/or a waste of your time.

> ❝You put your project management effort in where it will make a difference❞

Tracking the project

'Tracking the plan' means two things. It means (a) ensuring that what the plan says should be happening is happening; and (b) that what happens on the project is reflected in the plan.

The best way I know of doing this is to carry out the project manager's daily routine. It is by far the most efficient way I know of tracking a project. If you want to spend the least amount of time tracking your project and still have a successful outcome, then this is for you.

The project manager's daily routine

1 You come in in the morning and after your first little rituals of the day – coffee, chat with your friends, read the paper, etc. – you're ready to start. You sit down at your desk, take out your plan (or look at it on your computer screen) and do the following.

2 Look down the plan from top to bottom and identify any task that requires some action by you today.

3 Add these actions to your to-do list for today.

4 Do these actions.

5 For each task completed, record the results (actual work, actual start and end, actual duration) in the plan.

6 For each incident (unexpected event) that occurs on the project, determine whether or not it's a significant change according to the following table. (You'll recall from Chapter 2 that a significant change means that the basis upon which the plan was drawn up has changed and so the plan must be re-done.)

7 If the incident is not a significant change as determined by (6), update the plan with the incident.

	Significant change?	Use the contingency?	Do extra work?
1 The incident is a change to the scope of the project	Yes	No	No
2 The incident is not a change to the scope of the project but will require extra work	No	Yes	Yes, if you don't have contingency
3 Not sure whether it's a 1 or a 2	This will have to be resolved into either a 1 or a 2. It is here where most of your problems will occur. Something in the original scope of the project wasn't sufficiently well defined or specified. The stakeholders think it's in, you think it's out. You can certainly try to win some here. Be prepared to lose some. Whether you win or lose, learn from the experience. Tighten up your specifying/requirements-gathering process so that that particular thing could never happen again. If you religiously learn from your mistakes, then your project scoping will become very tight indeed. This in turn will tighten up your professionalism and improve your stakeholders' confidence in you.		
4 The incident represents a change to one of the assumptions in the plan	Yes	No	No
5 The incident is not a change to an assumption	No	Yes	Yes, if you don't have contingency

8 If the incident is a significant change as determined by (6), create a revised version of the plan and communicate this to the stakeholders. The stakeholders can then decide whether they want to go with this version of the plan or revert to the original plan.

9 Check to see whether the date and budget have changed. If they haven't, then the project is on target. If they have improved, say nothing. If they have dis-improved then this is a warning sign. A single dis-improvement by itself may not be a problem, since the slip could be corrected the next time you run the daily routine. But if, on several successive runnings of the daily routine, the trend is not in the right direction, this is a sign that you're in trouble. One way or other, you need to communicate the resulting status to the stakeholders.

Status reporting

A successful project is happy stakeholders. Happy stakeholders means setting and managing their expectations. Chapters 6 and 7 showed how to set those expectations initially. Status reporting manages those expectations over the life of the project.

"Happy stakeholders means setting and managing their expectations"

In general, people are interested in one or more of the following aspects of what you're doing:

- Will I get everything I thought I was going to get and if not, what can I expect?
- Is the project on time and if not, what can I now expect?
- How's it doing as regards costs? Over? Under? About right?
- Will the thing I get meet my needs?

In reporting the status, you need to tell them about which of these things they are interested in. And you need to tell them both the instantaneous status – here's how it is today – and what the status is over time – in other words, the trend. Only then can they have a true picture of how things are going. By truthfully reporting the trend, they can understand not just the kind of shape we're in today but how things might unfold in the future. The result of this will be that there are no surprises in store for anybody.

Here then is how to structure your status report. It needs to have three levels.

Level 1

Quite simply, is the project on target or not? Typically, your stakeholders are interested in either the delivery date or the budget or both. So tell the stakeholders just that. The project is on target to meet the delivery date or not. The project is within the budget or not.

Level 2

Here you need to explain how you got to be where you are. You need to give a change history – again of the delivery date and of the budget, if you're tracking it. Here's an example of a change history.

Date of change	Reason for change	Project end date
	Original date	1 Sep 2006
9 May 2006	Project scope changed at the request of the stakeholders	23 Jan 2007
27 May 2006	Added an extra person for a couple of weeks	12 Jan 2007
2 July 2006	Some improvements due to use of Mary	5 Jan 2007
14 Oct 2006	Slip in development schedule	19 Jan 2007

Level 3

Level 3 is the everything-and-the-kitchen-sink level. Here you can give them the current version of the plan, the current risk analysis and anything else that you fancy. If you want to write 'Tasks Completed Last Week/Tasks Planned for Next Week' you can do that. If you want to mention everybody on the team in dispatches and say who's working on what, you can do that. All of this is good stuff but it's nowhere near as important as what you put into levels 1 and 2.

Doing a post-mortem

If project management is about predicting the future and making that prediction come true, then project post-mortems (also known as project reviews, project audits or opportunities for improvement) are just about the best way to do that. In a project post-mortem you try to harvest knowledge from a completed project and then use that knowledge when you come to do your next project. There are three things you should look for.

> **❝In a project post-mortem you try to harvest knowledge from a completed project❞**

The completed plan

If you've updated your plan religiously as the project proceeded, then at the end of the project your plan will contain what actually happened. There will be no estimates in the plan now – everything will be fact. The information in the plan – how long things took, how much work went into jobs, how accurate your estimates were when compared with what actually happened – these things will be of immense value to you when you come to estimate (predict) your next project.

What did we do well?

Post-mortems tend to focus on what was done badly. (Maybe it's the gloomy connotations of the term 'post-mortem'.) While this is certainly valuable, it's also worth asking, 'What did you do well on this project?' Less is more here. Rather than an endless list of recommendations, few of which will probably be implemented, can you identify the one or two or three things that really made a difference on this project? What were these things? Figure out what they were and then share them with other parts of the organisation. One or two things may get acted on. A long list almost certainly won't.

> **"Can you identify the one or two or three things that really made a difference on this project?"**

What did we do badly?

It *is* a post-mortem, after all, so by all means then, what did you do badly? Again a handful of things. Again share them with the rest of the organisation.

Shortening your project

You'll remember in Chapter 3 about breaking the project down to a one-day level of detail and representing it on a spreadsheet. It may have seemed like a lot of work at the time. However, I hope you can see the additional benefit of it here, as running the project becomes childishly simple.

First of all it gives glaring visibility into who should be working on what on what day. This can be checked against reality on the ground. There is no uncertainty about deadlines. The spreadsheet is (depressingly!) clear about them. The targets for the week are obvious. Progress and slippage are both obvious.

But that's not all. As the project proceeds there is a whole bunch of things you can do to shorten the project. These are shown in the box below.

Ways to shorten your project further

1 Make every day count. In particular, don't do it tomorrow if it can be done today. 'Can I finish this today?'

2 Keep an eagle eye out for changes to the scope of the project.

3 If you find yourself waiting for somebody else, raise a flag so that something can be done about it.

4 If you're aware of a potential delay coming up, flag it as soon as it's known.

5 Keep dance cards up to date so that, at worst, you'll know if you have over-allocated yourself; at best, you may actually avoid over-allocating yourself altogether.

6 If you can start a job early, do so.

7 If you can finish a job early without compromising quality, do so.

8 If a piece of functionality can be achieved using a simpler or quicker approach, then do so.

CHAPTER 9

ASSESSING A PROJECT IN FIVE MINUTES

With the skills you have developed in Chapters 1–8, you now know how to plan and execute any project in the shortest possible time. This chapter and the next one extend your skills by giving you further techniques that you can use to save time on projects. This chapter shows you how to assess a project very quickly. You can use it in situations like the following:

- You are asked to take over a project that is already running.

- You are asked to assess a project.

- Somebody who reports to you is running a project – how do you know whether the project is in good shape?

- A sub-contractor does a presentation of their project plan. How do you know whether it is a good plan or not?

The project probability of success indicator (PSI)

The probability of success indicator (PSI) is a measurement you can take at any point in a project's life and it tells you how likely or not the project is to succeed.

> **"The probability of success indicator (PSI) is a measurement you can take at any point in a project's life"**

- If used at the beginning of a project, it becomes a practical approach/ checklist to gauge the probability of success before a project begins. Thus, it can stop turkey projects from getting off the ground.
- At any time, it will tell you whether a project is viable or not and identify the warning signs that the project is destined to fail.

How the PSI is measured

The PSI is measured by rating the project against the following criteria:

Criterion	Available score
1 How well defined or not is the goal?	20
2 Is there a final, definitive detailed list of jobs where every job has been broken down to the 1–5-day level of detail?	20
3 Does the project have somebody who, day to day, shepherds all of the jobs forward?	10
4 Are there people to do all of the jobs identified in 2? Do those people have enough time availability to devote to the project?	10
5 Is there contingency in the plan?	5
6 Has an up-to-date risk analysis been done and are the jobs to reduce those risks part of the project plan?	5
7 How much does the project manager vary their management style with the circumstances, micro-managing where necessary and hands off in other situations?	10
8 Is the project tracked on a regular basis? Never = 0; Daily = 10	10
9 Is there weekly *meaningful* status reporting?	10
Total	100

How to calculate the PSI

1 Goal

This is a measure of how well defined the goal is. The acid test here is that if you were to ask each stakeholder what the goal of the project is, and if each were to give you almost exactly the same reply, then the goal is well defined. Otherwise it is not. You only get a 20 when the project is complete because only then do you know exactly what was achieved. Pick a number between 0 and 20.

2 List of jobs

This is a measure of how complete the list of jobs is. Zero is no list. You might get 2 or 3 for a high level Work Breakdown Structure. You get 20 only when the project completes because only then do you know exactly what the list of jobs was. Pick a number between 0 and 20. If the goal (Step 1) scores low, then this will score low, since if you don't know what you're trying to do, how could you have a list of jobs to do it?

3 A leader

If the leader can be named and that person has adequate time available to run the project, then give 10, otherwise give 0.

4 People to do the jobs

If there aren't any/enough people to do the work, score this 0 or low. Also take into account that this step should be in the same proportion as Step 2, e.g. a 14/20 for Step 2 would give at most a 7/10 for Step 4.

5 Contingency

Allocate 5 for contingency. The more contingency, the higher the score out of 5.

6 Risk analysis

Allocate 5 for how well or badly the risk-reducing activities have been identified and are being carried out.

7 Management style

Pick a number between 0 and 10 based on how well the project manager varies their management style with the circumstances.

8 Project tracking

Pick a number between 0 and 10 based on how well the project manager uses the plan to steer the project. If the plan was thrown away as soon as the project was given the green light, score 0.

9 Status reporting

Pick a number between 0 and 10 based upon the regularity and adequacy of status reports.

How to interpret PSIs

If the goal isn't right, nothing will be right

If the goal isn't right, you miss one of the two opportunities to get a high score, but notice now how it all unravels. If you don't know what you're trying to do, creating a list of jobs to do it is impossible. (So too, it's worth noting, is setting the expectations of the stakeholders. If you don't know what you're trying to do, how could you set them? What will happen then is that everyone will set their own expectations.) Thus the list is flawed, resulting in missing the *other* opportunity to get a high score. If the list is flawed then it is impossible to lead the project properly (3) and it is equally impossible to assign people to the jobs (4). Contingency (5) and risk analysis (6) will have no meaning; 7 and 8 both require the job list and so a flawed job list causes these to fall apart as well.

60 is an important threshold

A PSI should start off low and rise steadily over the life of the project. Initially projects may not score more than 60 – this can just mean that there is more work to be done in terms of scoping the project (1) and planning it (2 through 6). However, a project should quickly go above 60 and stay above it. (Notice that the latter isn't guaranteed and a project can drop back again. This could happen, for example, if a major change to the scope of the project went uncontrolled.)

"A PSI should start off low and rise steadily over the life of the project"

Low scores always point you at the priority problem areas

Which is nice, I think you'll agree.

You can do anything you like on a poorly planned project and it won't make the blindest bit of difference

Chapter 7 mentioned Brooks' Law[2] – 'Adding people to a late project makes it later.' I believe that the above statement – 'you can do anything you like ...' – can be viewed as a generalisation of Brooks' Law. It basically says that if your project gets into difficulties, go back and look at the plan; don't just, for example, blindly ask everyone to work harder. The problem is in the plan, not in the execution of the plan.

Example of assessing a PSI

The following is based on a real project. Suppose you were faced with this problem. A project which is scheduled to take seventeen months has been running for eleven. There are about 250 people working on it. The project is extremely significant to the organisation and so a very senior person has been given the job of running it. There is lots of activity on the project. People are working long hours. Is the project in good shape or not?

Using your PSI checklist to guide you in your investigation you uncover the status given in column three of the following table. You then score the project as described in column four.

Criterion	Available score	Status	Actual score
1 How well defined or not is the goal?	20	Specifications for much of the project still don't exist even though the project is due to end in six months	Based on the proportion of specifications completed to those still not done, you score the project 14
2 Is there a final, definitive, detailed list of jobs where every job has been broken down to the 1–5-day level of detail?	20	Some parts of the project have plans, some parts have no plans. The bits that haven't been specified have no plans	Since only 70% (14/20) of the project is defined, this is the most that this could score. A 70% score would be possible if all the bits of the project that were specified had plans. However, some don't. Score this 10

Criterion	Available score	Status	Actual score
3 Does the project have somebody who, day to day, shepherds all of the jobs forward?	10	The very senior person still has all their other responsibilities, so they don't have anywhere near enough time to devote to a project of this magnitude. In addition, they see the day-to-day shepherding of the project as work that is really below them	This project doesn't have a leader. It has somebody with the title but nobody doing the job. Score 0
4 Are there people to do all of the jobs identified in 2? Do those people have enough time availability to devote to the project?	10	See 2	Since only 50% (10/20) of the jobs are identified, this could score no more than 50%. Give it 5
5 Is there contingency in the plan?	5	No	Score 0
6 Has an up-to-date risk analysis been done and are the jobs to reduce those risks part of the project plan?	5	No	Score 0

Criterion	Available score	Status	Actual score
7 How much does the project manager vary their management style with the circumstances, micro-managing where necessary and hands off in other situations?	10	See 3	Score 0
8 Is the project tracked on a regular basis? Never = 0; Daily = 10	10	See 3	Score 0
9 Is there weekly *meaningful* status reporting?	10	See 2, 3 and 8	Since there is no proper plan, status reporting has no meaning. Score 0
Total	100		29

"The project is in disastrous shape and is going nowhere"

Conclusion? The project is two-thirds of the way through its planned life and yet its PSI is well below 60. The project is in disastrous shape and is going nowhere. It has no chance of succeeding in its current form and will seriously overshoot its budget and its deadline. To rescue this project, the following need to be done in the order indicated:

1 Re-plan the project. (By including contingency in the plan and doing a risk analysis, scores 5 and 6 will both climb.)

2 Use the plan to re-set the expectations of the stakeholders. (This will not be a pleasant exercise.)

3 Complete the specifications. This will cause the 14/20 score to climb.

4 With the goal specified it will be possible to finalise the detailed list of jobs (causing the 10/20 to climb).

5 Now people will be working on the right things and everything else should start falling into place.

CHAPTER 10

SCOPING AND PLANNING A PROJECT IN A DAY

Why do it?

Projects can take a long time to get started. There is some kind of initial idea which gets worked up into a proposal which is then reviewed and updated a number of times until finally all of the stakeholders are happy. Then somebody works up a plan. This is also reviewed and updated a number of times; the proposal is probably modified again until eventually the final proposal and plan are ready. The process can take months – years, in some cases.

As an alternative to all of this, it is possible to scope and plan a project – even a very large one – in a day. You can be sceptical about this if you like, but I know it because I've done it – numerous times. I know it because my company, ETP, earns a sizeable proportion of its revenue from providing this very service.

To do it yourself on your projects all you need is this chapter. I apologise in advance that this chapter is so long and detailed, but I've tried to give you everything you need here to apply this very powerful technique. (The technique is illustrated in a description of an actual one-day scoping and planning session in Chapter 11.)

What's the overall approach?

There are two things that are the key to making this method work for you. The first is to bear in mind that your objective is to end the day with two deliverables – the scope document and the plan. The other is to spend the time as wisely as possible on the day to achieve these two deliverables.

> **"Your objective is to end the day with two deliverables – the scope document and the plan"**

So here – in broad terms – is how it works.

- You identify the people who are needed at the one-day scoping and planning session.
- There is preparation time before the one-day session. During this, attendees essentially prepare some of the input for the two documents mentioned above.
- At the one-day session, you act as facilitator and you need a second person to act as 'scribe'. During this session, the rest of the input is captured from the attendees and inserted into the documents.
- There is a tidying-up phase where the two documents are finalised. This generally amounts to little more than prettying them up.

Can anybody scope and plan a project in this way?

If you're capable of running a project, then you're capable of being a facilitator at one of these sessions. As for the scribe, she/he needs to know how to use Word, Excel, PowerPoint and MS Project (or their equivalents).

Preparation – what you need to get the attendees to do

- Identify all of the people who are entitled to a say in the scope of the project. This needs to include those people who sometimes don't necessarily appear high on the organisation chart, but who have the power to change everything at the stroke of a pen.

- Find a day when they can all come together. Make it clear to them that the sooner this can be, the sooner the project gets on the road. Explain to them that you're intending to scope and plan the project in a day and that this will get their project done quicker. Explain to them also that they will have to do some preparation beforehand, but that the benefit of doing this is that their project should be done quicker.

- Between the preparation and the one-day session, you are going to end up writing two documents. These are (a) a scope of the project, and (b) a plan for the project.

- Send the attendees a briefing note along the following lines:

Briefing note for participants in the scoping and planning session

The purpose of the session is to

1 Establish what the project is trying to achieve – 'the goal'.
2 Create a plan for reaching the goal.

The best way for individual participants to prepare for this is to try to do the following:

1 Document a goal for the project.
2 Prepare a plan to achieve this goal.

You should need no more than half a day to do this preparation and should limit yourself to whatever level of detail can be achieved in that time.

1 Goal

To do this, ask yourself questions like these. (Give yourself no more than an hour.)

- How will I know when the project is over?
- What will things be like? How will the company – or my piece of it – have changed?
- Who are the various people and/or groups ('the stakeholders') affected by the project?
- For each of these individuals or groups, what would constitute a successful project?
- Are these different views compatible? If not, is there a compromise set that we can live with?

2 Plan

To do this, do the following. (Plan to spend no more than 2–3 hours in total on the first three points and no more than an hour on the last two.)

- Make a list of all the jobs that you can think of that need to be done to reach *your piece* of the goal.
- Mark any dependencies between jobs (or dependencies on other projects or groups).
- Try to estimate how much work is involved in each job and therefore the project as a whole.

- Try to identify people who will do the work.
- Document any assumptions you make or unresolved issues you have.

"Document any assumptions you make or unresolved issues you have"

- Give them a deadline by when they need to get the stuff back to you. This deadline should be a day or two before the one-day session to allow you enough time to put together early drafts of the two documents.
- Using the material that comes back, start putting the two documents together, so that they can be used as a start point on the one-day session.
- If no material or only partial material comes back, don't panic – it can all still work on the day.

Preparation – what you need to do

Book a room that you're going to use for the one-day session. Ideally it should meet the following criteria:

- offsite
- plenty of light and windows – really important
- good ventilation/air conditioning
- walls to tape stuff to
- no telephones (or use of mobile phones allowed on the day)
- comfortable chairs and enough table/leg space for everybody
- refreshments available. Outside the room. Light lunch.

You will also need:

- a flipchart
- coloured markers (red, green, blue, black)
- LCD projector and screen
- a computer with Word, Excel, MS Project and PowerPoint (or their equivalents)
- a printer.

Closer to the one-day session, send round an e-mail giving attendees a bit more information about the day, especially the agenda. Here is the agenda for a 9–5 day.

09:00–10:45	Part 1 Establish the goal of the project – what would be the best possible outcome to this project?
10:45–11:00	Break
11:00–13:00	Part 2 Build the plan
13:00–13:45	Lunch
13:45–15:00	Part 2 Build the plan (continued)
15:00–15:15	Break
15:15–16:15	Part 3 Do a risk analysis on the plan – see where it can go wrong and what can be done to minimise the chances of that happening
16:15 – 17:00	Part 4 Assign next actions from the plan.

Running the session – Introduction

Welcome everybody. Introduce yourself and explain your role – you're going to run the session and keep everything on schedule. Introduce and explain the role of the scribe. She/he is going to record the proceedings so that the plan will be available at the end of the day.

Remind them of the agenda for the day.

Running the session – Part 1 09:00–10:45 Identify the goal of the project

You're going to do two things in Part 1. The first is to establish what will mark the end point of this project; the second is to identify the project's stakeholders and their win-conditions. Stakeholders are individuals or groups of people who are affected either positively or negatively by your project. Each stakeholder has what are called 'win-conditions'. Win-conditions are the things that would make a successful project for that particular stakeholder.

You want to devote roughly half an hour to establishing when this project will be over and about an hour to establishing the win-conditions of the stakeholders. The other fifteen minutes in the $1\frac{3}{4}$ hours devoted to Part 1 can be used as contingency.

To establish the goal of the project, there are two possible start points. If you got material back from the preparation phase, then you and the scribe will have put together a draft of the scope document. You can therefore begin by projecting this draft onto the screen. If you got nothing back, then your start point is a blank scope document.

Irrespective of your start point, these are the questions that you pose to the attendees at this point. 'How will we know when the project is over?' 'What point marks the end of the project?' The scribe will be adding the answers to the scope document.

"How will we know when the project is over?"

'Play back' the attendees' answers to them – 'So when this has happened and this has happened and this has happened, the project will be over, right?' 'So if all this happened, we would class the project as a success, yes?' Add the additional detail that flows from this.

Keep playing back their answers to them – 'So when this is done and this is done and this is done, then the project is over, right?' – until they all say yes. This needs to have taken you 30–45 minutes. (Note: if at this point you couldn't get agreement, you would have to call the session off. However, this has never happened to me in all the time I have been doing them.)

Once this is done, ask the attendees who all the stakeholders are. Write these down. Again, you may or may not have material from the preparation phase as a start point.

After this, and for each stakeholder, write down their win-conditions. The scribe writes in her/his document.

When they have run dry, play it back to them again. 'So this point in time we have chosen as the end of the project will deliver all these stakeholders' win-conditions?' If they agree then you're done. If not then there's more work to be done, either changing the point in time or modifying the win-conditions.

Keep at this until they agree that the point in time you have chosen as the end of the project delivers all of the stakeholders' win-conditions.

The combination, then, of the 'how will we know when it's over?' and the stakeholders' win-conditions gives you your final project scope. Or to put it another way, the point you have chosen as the end of your project should deliver all the win-conditions to the stakeholders.

The key to all of this is keeping the session running to time and doing as much as can be done in the time available. Here are a few things to help you:

- For the 'how will we know when it's over?' part of the session, you need to ensure that it finishes in or around half an hour.

- After that, it should be possible to make a list of the stakeholders in about ten minutes.

- You then have the best part of an hour to come up with the win-conditions. Think in terms of how many stakeholders there are and hence how much time you can devote to each. For ten stakeholders, you can give about five minutes to each of their win-conditions. For thirty stakeholders – yes, I've seen it! – you can devote only a minute or two.

- Finally, tell them that there'll only be a break when the Part 1 work has been done.

Once they have done all this work, you can give the attendees a break. Tie up with your scribe and make sure that you've captured everything. The document the scribe has is now the definition of the goal or the scope of the project. This project scope document can quite happily stand alone as the definition of the goal of the project. Alternatively, it can be used in documents such as project charters or project initiation documents.

❝The document the scribe has is now the definition of the goal or the scope of the project❞

Running the session – Part 2 11:00–15:00 Build the plan for the project

It's typically best to do this in MS Project. (Use task outline numbering in MS Project.) Once again, you may have material from the attendees so that you've already built a skeleton plan in MS Project. Otherwise you may be starting from a blank page.

Beam your start point onto the screen. Now ask the attendees to tell you the big phases of the project.

You have $3\frac{1}{4}$ hours to work on the plan. The number of big phases will guide you as to how much time you can devote to each phase and hence the level of detail that will be achievable. For, say, six big phases, you could devote about half an hour to each. If there were, say, ten big phases, you'd be down to about fifteen minutes each.

Once you have figured out how much time you can devote to each phase, you should probably reckon on using half that time to work out the detailed jobs in that phase. You will then use the other half of the time to estimate the duration of each of these detailed jobs.

Starting with the first big phase, begin to work out the detailed tasks. It may be useful to divide big phases into have-to-have/nice-to-have sub-phases.

Now take the first phase or sub-phase and figure out the first detailed job within that phase or sub-phase. Try to make the job as specific/ unambiguous/concrete as possible, e.g. rather than saying 'requirements gathering' say 'Charlie meets with the IT people for two days to explain his requirements'. If you find you cannot make the task unambiguous, it means you need to add another level of detail.

Be conscious of the time limit you've set yourself for each big phase. It may be that you can only go to a certain level of detail in that time.

That's ok. Keep doing the previous step at the level of detail you've chosen until you have completed that phase. You need to have done it pretty much within the time limit you've set yourself, i.e. using the first half of the time devoted to each phase.

Now, using the other half of the time devoted to each phase, put in names against the jobs and estimate durations.

You may have to make assumptions along the way as you do this, e.g. not knowing, for instance, how many testing/fixing phases there are going to be in your project, you may have to make an assumption, so that you can build the detail. That's completely OK.

In terms of keeping things on schedule, the following are all good:

- Try to get about two-thirds of the phases done before the lunch break and don't go to lunch with a phase partially completed.

- Use the times allocated to each of the big phases as little milestones to keep yourself on target. Once you've run out of time in a particular phase, approximate anything that remains (using assumptions) and then move on to the next phase.

- This is really important – don't get bogged down in things. You're trying to build sequences of jobs, not carry out the jobs themselves. Techies are particularly prone to talking about things like design alternatives or technologies to be used. That's not the purpose of this meeting. You want to build sequences of jobs. If they say they can't do that without knowing which of two alternative technologies is going to be used, for example, make an assumption one way or the other and push on. Anything that isn't related to building the sequence of jobs should be moved offline.

“Don't get bogged down in things”

Once you've finished this process for all the big phases, you're done – you've got your basic plan.

Two other things to do before you give the attendees a break. One is to put contingency into the plan. Add some additional time onto the end date of the project. This is to cover unexpected events that might occur over the life of the project. If you're looking for a rule of thumb, maybe add 15% of the duration of the project. In other words, if the project lasts seven months, add a month for contingency. The other thing to do is to estimate the amount of project management the project will need. Do this as described in Chapter 3.

Running the session – Part 3 15:15–16:15 Do a risk analysis on the project

Now, do a risk analysis on the project as described in Chapter 5. There shouldn't really be any problem with getting this done in an hour.

Running the session – Part 4 16:15–17:00 Allocate next actions

Reading from the newly created plan, assign next actions to session attendees. As an alternative to this, you could just say to the attendees, 'Look at the plan to see what you've got to get done in the next week. Let's meet back here a week from today to see if all these things got done.' If you choose to do that, just schedule the next meeting and then you can actually end the day *ahead* of schedule. (So, in fact, with the schedule we've given here there's actually a little contingency at the end of the day, if you need it. But just to reiterate, what makes this process work is that you make all those intermediate little milestones you set yourself.)

You're done!

"What makes this process work is that you make all those intermediate little milestones you set yourself"

Tidying up the one-day session

You can give the copies of the scope document and the plan to your attendees at the end of the day. There may, however, be some tidying and prettying up of the two documents to be done. The scribe should do this first thing the following day and have them out to the attendees later that day. However, this shouldn't stop the attendees from using the rougher versions from the end of the previous day's one-day session to go off and start doing their tasks on the project.

CHAPTER 11

AN ACTUAL SCOPING AND PLANNING SESSION

The goal of the project

To give you an even better sense of what a one-day scoping and planning session might be like, this section and the one that follows describe pieces of an actual scoping and planning session.

This example session is about a project to develop a product. As it happens the product is a software product, positioned vaguely in the financial services area. The fact that it's software is unimportant. Everyone understands products and that they get developed. Everyone also understands that products have features and so too does this one. However, the set of features that makes up this product doesn't necessarily make sense as a real product. It doesn't matter. What was needed was a reasonable size project to illustrate the ideas, one that would be big enough to seem convincing but not so big that it would be overwhelming.

"Everyone understands products and that they get developed"

This section describes the 'goal of the project' part of the session; the next section describes the 'plan for the project' part. I haven't included the risk analysis part of the one-day session (though the risk analysis itself is the example given in Chapter 5). Also the next actions part would be self-evident from the plan that was developed.

The example, then, concerns the development of a software product for the financial services industry. Here's a little more flesh to that basic scenario.

The company decides that it is going to develop a new product. The board says 'the share price has been languishing. The company needs a new killer product'. The CEO says 'there's a window of opportunity and we're the people to go for it'. Finance say 'the product must have high margins and bring in this much profit over the next whatever'. Marketing say 'it's gotta beat these features that our competitor's products have'. In the time-honoured tradition, sales announce the product, say 'it will demo at a trade show with general availability a few weeks later', and answer 'yes' any time a customer or potential customer asks whether it will have the blah feature. Engineering say 'the product has to run on these platforms, have these features, be web-enabled [whatever that might mean] and have all these other techno-babble features as well'. In this and the section which follows I've assumed that you're the project manager!

You decide to scope and plan this project in a day. You manage to get all of the right people together. You have given them their preparation to do, but the response has been fairly patchy, so essentially you're starting from a blank page. They arrive in the room, with looks ranging from expectancy to irritation. Your scribe is sitting at the back, poised over his computer. You ask the first big question.

You: 'How will we know when this project is over?'

Engineering: 'The product is out the door.'

CEO: 'It's selling in droves.'

Finance: 'It has added $5 million to the bottom line [Pause] in year 1.'

Marketing: 'When the reviews say it's the best of breed.'

Sales: 'When it demos at the trade show [in case you'd forgotten!]. No, no. When the [thousands of] orders we take at the trade show have shipped.'

You: 'Which?'

A general discussion ensues. You guide them to the conclusion that all of these points might constitute possible endings of the project. And that in fact what these different endings give you is your first cut of what we have called the 'big phases'. These various points are milestones in the life of the project, which might look something like this.

1 Start.

2 Product demos at the trade show.

3 Product leaves engineering.

4 Product reviews occur.

5 End of year 1 revenues.

You: 'So what constitutes its end point?'

Again you lead them to the notion that all of these are valid end points, depending on your point of view. What is of concern to you today is that you pick one that you can all buy into and work with. More discussion. The group finally makes the following choices, but notice that they are precisely that – choices – which means you could have chosen differently and still be correct.

1 The group decides that the year 1 revenues one is too far away to really think about.

2 Next it decides that while reviews are important, what's more important is that those first users of the product like it. It's clear that those people who buy the product at the trade show will be its first users and so you revise your milestones like this.

  1 Start.

  2 Product demos at the trade show.

  3 Test version of the product leaves engineering and ships to the trade show buyers. (A test period follows during which customers are closely monitored and supported, errors and requests

for changes are reported, and engineering fix some while adding others to the Release 2 wish list.)

4 Test period ends when (a) no more major errors exist and (b) at least 50% (the number is chosen arbitrarily) of customers have ordered more copies.

5 End.

3 You make a final decision whose sole purpose it is to make this current example more manageable. You decide that for your present purposes, you will treat the end of the project as the day on which the test version leaves engineering. Marketing is happy with that.

❝You make a final decision whose sole purpose it is to make this current example more manageable❞

Marketing: 'Don't worry. You let us worry about the test programme. We've done dozens of these before. You just get the product to us as quickly as you can and we'll take it from there.'

You (looking the marketing guy right in the eye): 'So the test programme will be the subject of a separate plan?'

Marketing: 'Yes.'

You write this down on a sheet of flipchart paper that you label 'Actions'. It has three columns – what, who, when. It reads '1 Develop test plan/Marketing guy/To be filled in [ideally before you leave the room]'. The list of milestones now reads:

1 Start.

2 Product demos at the trade show.

3 Test version of the product leaves engineering.

4 End.

Next question.

You: 'As part of trying to figure out when the project is over, can we say what physical things the project will produce?'

Let's assume you get to the answers without too much difficulty and that the list of deliverables is:

- the software itself – in a form whereby it can be distributed
- user manual
- online tutorial.

You: 'Anything else?'

There follows much discussion. Eventually you settle on the following. You will build a prototype that marketing will show to some users to get feedback. There will be reviews of the requirements and designs. A separate group will test the product and they will be the people who decide whether the product is fit to go into the customer test programme. The prototype is considered important enough that it is added to the list of milestones.

1 Start.

2 Prototype available.

3 Product demos at the trade show.

4 Test version of the product leaves engineering as soon as internal testing completes.

5 End.

You: 'Can we say something about the functionality that will be delivered when the project is completed?'

This is the part of the show where everyone gets a chance to talk about features and the attendees go at it for all they're worth. Eventually you end up with ten features (your product is going to be small and elegant and containing what you believe to be killer features):

1 Pricing.

2 Foreign exchange.

3 Euro support.

4 Third-party payments.

5 Settlement.

6 Reporting.

7 Web interface.

8 Security.

9 Tutorial.

10 Online help.

For good measure, engineering throw in the operating environment the system will run in and software engineering environment that they will use to build the product. Also they make the point that this will be an English language-only version. They do this to wind up the marketing guy, who promptly obliges by leaping out of his seat and saying that the product has to be available in French, Italian, German, Spanish – oh, and Japanese, Chinese, Thai and Indonesian. A bit of a tussle ensues in which the marketing guy restates his case and engineering just keep saying 'you want it when?'. What is eventually agreed is that this release will be English only. However, it will contain all the facilities necessary for multilingual support. The actual availability in the other languages will follow as part of Release 2.

You: 'And that's it – nothing else? We now have our scope?'

They sort of agree.

'Training course?' you ask.

There's a bit of a row, but eventually it's agreed that there will be no training course – the tutorial is considered to be adequate. A whole list of features that marketing had hoped to get included also get battered into Release 2.

'So, ok,' you say, finally summarising. 'If we were to

- get these ten features [you show them the feature list]
- out the door in this kinda timeline [you show them the list of milestones]
- with these deliverables [you show them the list of deliverables]
- in English only,

then everybody would be happy?'

A reasonably lengthy silence follows, which is broken when the sales guy says, 'As long as it was within thirty days of the trade show.' You repeat your assertion with the desired amendment. Ok, so

- get these ten features [you show them the feature list]
- out the door in this kinda timeline [you show them the list of milestones]
- with these deliverables [you show them the list of deliverables]
- in English only
- and within thirty days of the trade show,

then everyone would be happy. There is nodding and general agreement. You're there. You remind them one more time that this is the plan for the engineering part of the project only and that other plans will be required for the other bits – marketing, sales, etc. They all nod, you add to your action list precisely which plans will be needed.

You: 'Now, one more thing before we stop for a break. We're going to make a list of all the stakeholders and their win-conditions.'

"We're going to make a list of all the stakeholders and their win-conditions"

You start with the stakeholders:

Stakeholder	
The shareholders	
The board	
The CEO	
The customers	
The heads of marketing, sales, engineering	
You (the project manager)	
The team	

Now you add each stakeholder's win-conditions.

Stakeholder	Win-conditions
The shareholders	● Grow market share ● Meet profit targets
The board	● Grow market share ● Meet profit targets ● Make them look good
The CEO	● Grow market share ● Meet profit targets ● Make him look good
The customers	● Good-quality product ● Solves a real need for them, i.e. adds value
The heads of marketing, sales, engineering	● Grow market share ● Meet profit targets ● Make them look good ● Help them to keep their jobs
You (the project manager)	● An interesting piece of work ● Make you look good ● You keep your job
The team	● Interesting work ● Make them look good

When the list is complete, you ask whether the project, as scoped in the previous section, meets all of these conditions. It is generally agreed that it does, provided that the sales and marketing plans are also developed and rolled into the equation. Notice again how crucial this is. (Remember that I removed sales and marketing from the equation only to limit the scope of this example and to enable it to fit within the confines of this chapter. Had you been doing this for real, you would almost certainly *not* have excluded these two areas from the project scope – if for no other reason that than having asked the relevant people along, it would then have been fairly outrageous to exclude them from the proceedings.) Without these two other plans, notice that the number of stakeholders whose win-conditions are satisfied is hugely reduced. Without them, the only people whose win-conditions might potentially have any chance of being satisfied would be those of the head of engineering, you, the project manager, and the team. I say 'might' because you might produce the greatest product the world had ever seen, but if sales and marketing didn't do their bits, the product might only be remembered as a turkey.

Anyway, back to the session. It is generally agreed that provided sales and marketing can scope their projects as effectively as the engineering plan has just been scoped, all of the stakeholders' win-conditions would be satisfied. It's time to give them a break and then move on to planning the project.

The plan for the project

Now, with the project scoped, you are ready to begin the planning. What you will do first is to identify jobs, dependencies and effort. You will then add in people and their availability. In what follows, the working out of the jobs, dependencies and effort has been described in complete detail. For the people and their availability, only the result is shown. This is in the interests of keeping this example (a) interesting and useful, but also (b) of manageable proportions.

❝What you will do first is to identify jobs, dependencies and effort❞

For the jobs, dependencies and effort, you will end up building the plan that is shown in Figure 11.1 (the full version can be seen in the appendix on page 138).

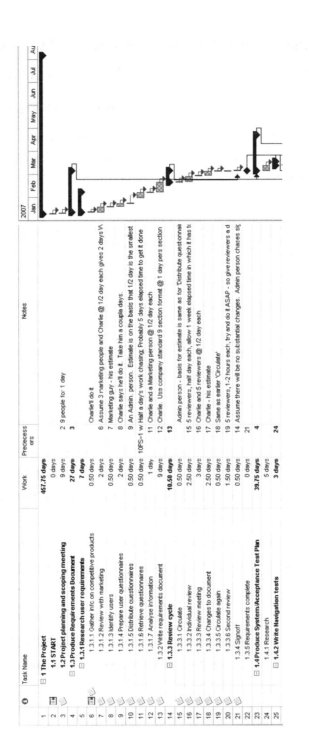

Figure 11.1 Plan with jobs, dependencies and effort

Here's how you do it.

You (nodding to your scribe who writes down the words ' START'): 'Ok, who does what? What happens first?'

'This meeting,' somebody pipes up. You nod to your scribe and he does the necessary, adding in the fact that the meeting is a day elapsed, but given that there are nine participants (you, scribe, CEO, marketing guy, sales guy, engineering guy, a couple of other engineers, finance guy), it is nine days' effort.

Now the marketing guy puts a spanner in the works by saying that they need to survey potential users and competitive products. You groan inwardly. You assumed they would have done this prior to this meeting. Otherwise how could the marketing input be valid? Tactfully, you say nothing, but begin to put in place the sequence of events that will fold in (a) the input from today, (b) the results of the competitive analysis, and (c) the user questionnaires into a requirements document.

You: 'What happens next?'

'Gather info on competitive products?'

'Any idea of an estimate?'

'Half a day on the net should do it,' mutters Charlie, one of the engineers. 'If I do it,' he adds. You accept his offer – even if it wasn't intended as one.

'Next?'

'Review the stuff with marketing.'

'Estimate?'

You note (in the Notes field) what they intend to do and move on. For the next few lines the Notes field shows the conclusions you come to.

'That's gonna need a review cycle,' you say, once you've covered '1.3.2 Write requirements document.' Everyone agrees, so you throw in exactly that. Again you put in the Notes field the estimates associated with the various tasks. So now we're starting to make some progress. 'What's next?' you ask.

'Well, once we've got the requirements,' says the other engineering type – Charlie's buddy, Engineer #2 – 'given the level of detail we do requirements at in this organisation, we'll be able to write an acceptance test plan.' Engineer #2 is one of those people who, if you asked them what time it was, would tell you how to build a watch. He does this somewhat now. 'So,' he continues, 'we'll have to do some kinda research first. Then we'll have to do navigation, functionality, integrity, performance, stress and installation tests.' Your scribe is writing furiously. Engineer #2 finishes. You say, 'And so, Engineer #2, give us the estimates.' Engineer #2 is stumped for a moment, before resorting to the age-old fallback of software people when asked for an estimate. 'I dunno,' he says, 'how long is a piece of string?' But you're not buying this. You push a little harder. 'For each type of test, what do we have to do, Engineer #2?' Engineer #2 hesitates before continuing. 'Define the tests ... write the scripts ... define the test data and expected results.' You nod encouragingly, drawing him on. Your scribe scribes. 'Estimates, Engineer #2?' Engineer #2 is either going to get very angry with you or wrestle with the problem. He is like a train coming up to a set of points. The points click. He goes down the wrestle-with-the-problem line. 'I really don't know,' he says. 'How about assume one day's work for each of the three aspects and do as much as you can in that day.' You can't really come up with a better idea yourself, so you go with that. You throw in a review cycle and a signoff. That's it for the system/acceptance test plan.

You feel you're starting to get onto a bit of a roll. 'Next up?' 'High-level design,' the engineering people chorus. You propose going at it the same way as the previous two documents, the requirements and system test plan. But Engineer #2 says, 'Aw, didn't we say we'd do a prototype?'

'Sure,' you say, 'it's a good way to go.' Addressing the other occupants in the room, you say, 'What Engineer #2 and Charlie are essentially saying – correct me if I picked you up wrong, guys – is that there's a lot to be said for adopting the we'll know it when we see it approach. So that instead of writing and reviewing a document, we'll build a proto-type, let you guys review it, change it, review it again and so on. Let's be clear, too, that this is not just a mock-up of the user interface, but that the underlying design concepts, structure, architecture will be worked out. That right, guys?' They nod. To do that you would then have a sequence of jobs that went

1 Build prototype.
2 Review with marketing and note changes.
3 Go back to 1.

"There's a lot to be said for adopting the we'll know it when we see it approach"

'So can you estimate this for us, guys? Say five days for the first build, a day to review. Now a second iteration … and a third iteration … assuming eight iterations.' You have scribbled something on the flipchart that looks like this (see opposite).

'What makes you think it'll only be eight iterations?' asks Engineer #2. 'We're *assuming* it's eight iterations, Engineer #2,' you say. 'It can be any number you like. Do you think it should be more? Less?'

Job/Iteration	1	2	3	4	5	6	7	8	Totals
1 Build/revise prototype	5	3	2	2	2	1	1	1	17
2 Review with marketing	1	1	0.5	0.5	0.5	0.5	0.5	0.5	5
Total per iteration	6	4	2.5	2.5	2.5	1.5	1.5	1.5	22

All estimates in person-days

'Leave it at eight for the moment.'

'Let's put in one line item,' you say. 'Prototype, twenty-two days' effort. And note that as well as assuming eight iterations, we're assuming people are available immediately to review the work. So the twenty-two days' effort is also twenty-two days' elapsed time.' You call a break.

After the break, the group reassembles and you move on. The next milestone you identified earlier was the demo at the trade show. It is now agreed that the prototype will constitute the demo. Marketing will take the final prototype resulting from iteration eight and make it the basis for the demo. It will be their job to get it to the trade show and it is agreed that that project is outside the scope of this one. Marketing asks to have Charlie or Engineer #2 on hand during the trade show and this is agreed.

'Who does what next?' you ask. 'Code,' Engineer #2 says. 'Ok,' you say, 'let's estimate it.' 'Won't know till we've done the design – eh, the proto type,' says Charlie. You say, 'We have ten features, right?' You write them down on the left-hand side of a flipchart page.

1 Pricing.

2 Foreign exchange.

3 Euro support.

4 Third-party payments.

5 Settlement.

6 Reporting.

7 Web interface.

8 Security.

9 Tutorial.

10 Online help.

General agreement. 'Are they all the same size and complexity?' General agreement that they aren't – necessarily. 'So can we try to figure out which is which?' Nodding. 'Could we maybe rate them according to some scheme or other?' Nodding. 'How about this? We'll class them as small (S), medium (M) or large (L) and then try to estimate them?' More nodding. Also some scepticism. Still, there seems to be a general air of 'it can't hurt'. You run down the list and people propose their various views. There is good discussion because often what marketing had in mind for a particular feature bears no relation to what engineering were intending to do. All the decisions about what a particular feature is or isn't get recorded in your notes from the scoping part of the day. You finally end up with your flipchart page looking like this.

1 Pricing (S).

2 Foreign exchange (M).

3 Euro support (M).

4 Third-party payments (M)

5 Settlement (S).

6 Reporting (S).

7 Web interface (L).

8 Security (L).

9 Tutorial (M).

10 Online help (L).

"All the decisions about what a particular feature is or isn't get recorded in your notes"

'Ok, now for each of these items, what jobs do we have to do?' You flip the flipchart page, reorder the features and draw a table. 'Write Code, Document Code, Test Code?' somebody suggests. It sounds reasonable enough.

Feature	Size	Write code	Document code	Test code
Pricing	S			
Settlement	S			
Reporting	S			
Foreign exchange	M			
Euro support	M			
Third-party payments	M			
Tutorial	M			
Web interface	L			
Security	L			
Online help	L			

'Estimates?' you ask briskly. 'We'd only be guessing,' says Engineer #2, earnestly. 'Guess away,' you say. They do. Occasionally you question an estimate and when in doubt you always increase it. Again there is discussion about the way particular features will appear or will be implemented, but you try to keep this brief. That's not really what you're attempting to do today. You propose a couple of assumptions, namely that you will assume that a medium feature takes twice as long to code as a small one, and that a large feature takes three times as long. (The value of doing this is that if, when you run the project, the first three features you code are a small, a medium and a large one, you can soon see how valid this assumption was. This in turn acts as a form of early warning about your estimates.) You plug in a job sequence for the testing, and estimating its individual components makes you more comfortable with the overall estimate. For the large components, you assume that when they come to be done, each will break down into four major elements which have to get done. (The value of doing this is again to do with early warning. If, when the prototype has been done and the design is clear, it turns out that the large components are much larger than you anticipated (e.g. one of them has ten major components, not four), then you again know that there may be a problem with your estimates.)

Finally your table looks like this.

Feature	Size	Assumption	Write code	Document code	Test code	Totals
Pricing	S		4	0.5	3.5	8
Settlement	S		4	0.5	3.5	8
Reporting	S		4	0.5	3.5	8
Foreign exchange	M	M = 2S	8	1	7	16
Euro support	M	M = 2S	8	1	7	16
Third-party payments	M	M = 2S	8	1	7	16
Tutorial	M	M = 2S	8	1	7	16
Web interface	L	L = 3S	12	4	16	32
Security	L	L = 3S	12	4	16	32
Online help	L	L = 3S	12	4	16	32

All estimates in person-days

You're going to need a technical author to work on this project, but that person hasn't been identified yet and there's nobody in the room with a background in that discipline. All you can do is try as best you can. You ask the question. 'So what happens next?'

Somebody fronts up with another 'Research' and you happily accept this. The two jobs that follow it are pure guesses. Still, your take on it is this. If push came to shove, somebody could just write the text in Word, pretty it up and send it out. These ten person-days may or may not be needed. At worst they are, at best it's a bit more contingency.

The four jobs under 'Write user documentation or Help text' are again guesses. You notice that there's going to be a large amount of overlap between the feature 'Online help' and these jobs. There are issues to be sorted out there. For example, can the technical author write one lot of text that can be used in both the user manual and the online help? It seems likely. If so, there could be a great heap of contingency buried inside these jobs. However, you judge correctly that it's something you don't have to waste everybody's time with today. You slap down your estimates and press on. You can smell the finish line.

Somebody pipes up about editing and integrating the user documentation and help text. Another five jobs spatter onto the plan. Again, these can be cleaned up later. The final act in the drama is the system testing. You suggest an assumption that three passes will be enough. You make a couple of assumptions to enable you to estimate the first pass and then you scale down the estimates for the other two iterations. An end-of-project review completes the show.

"An end-of-project review completes the show"

The people to do the work, those people's availability and the resulting durations would be added to the plan in exactly the same way. They would result in Figures 11.2 (see Appendix for full version) and 11.3.

#	Task Name	Work	Predecessors	Resource Names	Duration
1	1 The Project	610 days			154 days
2	1.1 START	0 days			0 days
3	1.2 Project planning and scoping meeting	9 days	2		1 day
4	1.3 Produce Requirements Document	27 days	3		39.50 days
5	1.3.1 Research user requirements	7 days			19.50 days
6	1.3.1.1 Gather info on competitive products	0.50 days		Charlie	0.50 days
7	1.3.1.2 Review with marketing	2 days	6	Analyst #1 [20	5 days
8	1.3.1.3 Identify users	0.50 days	7	Marketing guy	0.50 days
9	1.3.1.4 Prepare user questionnaires	2 days	8	Charlie	2 days
10	1.3.1.5 Distribute questionnaires	0.50 days	9	Administrative	0.50 days
11	1.3.1.6 Retrieve questionnaires	0.50 days	10FS+1 w	Administrative	5 days
12	1.3.1.7 Analyse information	1 day	11	Analysts	1 day
13	1.3.2 Write requirements document	9 days	12	Charlie	9 days
14	1.3.3 Review cycle	10.50 days	13		10.50 days
15	1.3.3.1 Circulate	0.50 days		Administrative	0.50 days
16	1.3.3.2 Individual review	2.50 days	15	Requirements	5 days
17	1.3.3.3 Review meeting	3 days	16		0.50 days
18	1.3.3.4 Changes to document	2.50 days	17	Charlie	2.50 days
19	1.3.3.5 Circulate again	0.50 days	18	Administrative	0.50 days
20	1.3.3.6 Second review	1.50 days	19		0.50 days
21	1.3.4 Signoff	0.50 days	14	Administrative	0.50 days
22	1.3.5 Requirements complete	0 days	21		0 days
23	1.4 Produce System/Acceptance Test Plan	40 days	4		33.00 days
24	1.4.1 Research	5 days		Tester #1	5 days
25	1.4.2 Write Navigation tests	3 days	24		3 days
26	1.4.2.1 Define test sequence	1 day		Tester #1	1 day
27	1.4.2.2 Write test scripts	1 day	26	Tester #1	1 day
28	1.4.2.3 Define expected results	1 day	27	Tester #1	1 day

Gantt timeline (2007 / 2008 / 2009) annotations: Tue 9/1/07; Charlie; Analyst #1 [20%],Marketing people [20%]; Marketing guy; Charlie; Administrative Assistant; Administrative Assistant [10%]; Analysts; Charlie; Administrative Assistant; Requirements Reviewer [50%]; Charlie; Administrative Assistant; Administrative Assistant; Tue 6/3/07; Tester #1; Tester #1; Tester #1; Tester #1

Figure 11.2 Final plan

		Charlie	Engineer #2	Engineer #3	Engineer #4	Technical author	Marketing people (3)	Admin Assistant	Reqs. Reviewers (5)	Test & Design Reviewers (2)	Tester #1	Tester #2	Users	Project Management
1	09-Jan-07	3 Proje				3 Project planning and scoping m		3 Project planning and scoping meeting						3 Project planning and scopir
2	10-Jan-07	6 Gathe												
3	11-Jan-07	9 Prepare user questionnaires												
4	12-Jan-07	9 Prepare user questionnaires						10 Distribute user questionnaires						
5	15-Jan-07													
6	16-Jan-07	7 Review with Marketing					7 Review with Marketing							
7	17-Jan-07													
8	18-Jan-07													
9	19-Jan-07								11 Retrieve questionnaires					
10	22-Jan-07	12 Analyse information												
11	23-Jan-07	13 Write requirements document												
12	24-Jan-07	13 Write requirements document												
13	25-Jan-07	13 Write requirements document												
14	26-Jan-07	13 Write requirements document												
15	29-Jan-07	13 Write requirements document												
16	30-Jan-07	13 Write requirements document												
17	31-Jan-07	13 Write requirements document												
18	01-Feb-07	13 Write requirements document												
19	02-Feb-07	13 Write requirements document												
20	05-Feb-07								15 Circulate document					
21	06-Feb-07													
22	07-Feb-07													
23	08-Feb-07													
24	09-Feb-07								16 Individual review[1/2 day each]					
25	12-Feb-07	17,18,19 Review meeting / changes to document (inc. circula						17 Review meeting [1/2 day]						
26	13-Feb-07	17,18,19 Review meeting / changes to document (inc. circulate again)												
27	14-Feb-07	17,18,19 Review meeting / changes to document (inc. circulate again)												
28	15-Feb-07	20-22 Second review / Signoff / Reqs complete [1/4	18-20 Se		18-20 Second review / Signoff / Reqs complete [1/4 day]									

Figure 11.3 Strip board with jobs added from Gantt Chart

CHAPTER 12

WHY PROJECTS FAIL

Pretty much everyone has their favourite failed project story. One of my own particular favourites was from a few years back. It concerned a DSS information system in Britain that was originally intended to cost £2.75 billion, but would result in a net saving of 2,000 jobs. Eventually, with the project way off target, an enquiry had determined that the system would cost *at least* another £750 million to finish and that employment in the DSS had actually gone *up*.

The thing I find most extraordinary about this project is that I can't remember the name of it and generally, when I mention it to other people, neither can they. You would be inclined to think that a foul-up on this scale would be remembered and go down in the annals among the world's greatest foul-ups. Incredibly that's not the case – which just goes to show how routine such foul-ups have become. What's most amazing about this project is the way it's *not* remembered.

Every day it seems people involved in projects wake to find themselves in a mess. As the French general Ducrot put it most colourfully after the Battle of Sedan: *'Nous sommes dans un pot de chambre et nous y serons emmerdés.'*

It doesn't have to be like this. It doesn't have to be like this if only people would stop making the same mistakes over and over again. Project management is not rocket science. In fact, it is anything but. Projects go wrong because people don't do the things discussed in the first eight chapters of this book. This final chapter has been put here just to remind you what can happen if you try to pretend that the first eight chapters don't apply to you! If this book so far has been about fast projects, this chapter is about slow, painful and doom-laden projects.

"Project management is not rocket science. In fact, it is anything but"

The Dirty Dozen

Here, then, are the top reasons why projects fail.

1 The project was never actually possible in the first place.

2 The goal of the project wasn't defined properly.

3 The goal of the project was defined properly, but then changes to it weren't controlled.

4 Stakeholders and/or stakeholders' win-conditions weren't identified.

5 The project was planned properly, but then it wasn't resourced as planned.

6 The project was planned, but with no contingency.

7 The project wasn't planned properly.

8 The project wasn't led properly.

9 The expectations of project participants weren't managed.

10 The project was planned properly, but then progress against the plan was not monitored properly.

11 Project reporting was inadequate or non-existent.

12 When the project got into trouble, people believed the problem could be solved by some simple action, e.g. work harder, extend the deadline, add more resources.

1 The project was never actually possible in the first place

In my experience this is the most common reason for project failure. Somebody says, 'Here's the project, we don't know much about it, but it has to be done by this date for this budget,' and everybody says, 'OK.' If you only took one idea away from this book, it should be that when somebody does hand you a project, instead of saying 'OK,' you say, 'I'll take a look at it.' You 'take a look at it' using the methods in Chapters 1–5, then you commit only to doing something that's possible, as described in Chapters 6 and 7.

2 The goal of the project wasn't defined properly

This has been said so many times, beginning right back in Ancient Rome ('If you don't know what port you're sailing to, then any wind is a fair wind' – Pliny), that it has become a platitude, but it is as true now as it ever was. Look at the Taurus project in the London Stock Exchange about fifteen years ago. The day after its collapse, the Chairman of the Stock Exchange said in the *Financial Times*, 'We were testing parts of the system while other parts hadn't been designed or built.' And they wondered why it had gone wrong! Chapters 2 and 10 tell you how to figure out the goal of your project.

3 The goal of the project was defined properly, but then changes to it weren't controlled

The moving goalposts syndrome. The famous project management phrase is 'we've absorbed that into the schedule'. *Nothing* can be absorbed into the schedule. If your plan has some contingency in it, then you can *appear* to do that, but what you are actually doing is spending a part of your contingency. If your plan has no contingency in it, then all you are really doing is joining the 'it'll be alright on the day' school of project management.

Remember Chapter 2 and Chapter 8 about the three possible responses to changes on a project:

- Declare it to be a significant change (and revise the plan accordingly).
- Use the contingency to cover the change.
- Work longer hours to cover the change.

Don't habitually just do the third one.

4 Stakeholders and/or stakeholders' win-conditions weren't identified

If you don't know who all the stakeholders are, the chances of you delivering a result that makes them happy are pretty remote. Equally, if you fail to identify win-conditions, the chances of you delivering those win-conditions by accident are remote. Chapter 2 is about capturing all the stakeholders and win-conditions.

5 The project was planned properly, but then it wasn't resourced as planned

I've seen projects which were meant to be finished in a year last four years because of this. It's a dangerous one because the slip is so gradual. Sloppy monitoring of the plan (see (10) below) will make it even more difficult to track. You *must* allow for people's other commitments when you build your plan around them. Chapter 4 described the dance card as a way of doing this.

> ❝Sloppy monitoring of the plan will make it even more difficult to track❞

6 The project was planned, but with no contingency

If you build your plan without contingency, then the only logical conclusion one can come to is that you believe your project will turn out exactly like your plan says. Now, of all the things that might happen, this *has* to be the least likely. Yet in putting no contingency into the plan, this is precisely what you're saying *will* happen.

Also, if there is no contingency in your plan, every change that occurs on the project that is not a significant change will have to be covered by you and your team working more hours. Chapter 5 describes how to put contingency in the plan.

7 The project wasn't planned properly

Project planning is the act of chaining together all the myriad little jobs that go to make up the project ('building the sequence of events'). A proper plan attempts to do this chaining together as early in the project as possible. If this isn't done, there are only two other ways the chaining together can happen. The first is that it is done in real time – this is the firefighting project manager, where everything is unexpected, a surprise, a crisis. The second is that it is not done at all – this is the go-with-the-flow, it'll-be-alright-on-the-day approach. We've all seen too often the effects of the last two approaches. Chapters 1–5 are about building a proper plan.

8 The project wasn't led properly

For the project to be successful, all the jobs identified in the plan need to be done. One person – the project manager – has to make sure that this happens. Note, in particular, that this includes jobs which aren't necessarily being done by 'our' people, i.e. those jobs being done by management, the customer, other departments, suppliers, sub-contractors and so on. Chapter 3 shows how to make sure that time is set aside for project management and describes your responsibilities.

9 The expectations of project participants weren't managed

People often say, 'In our company deadlines are imposed on us.' They say this as though they had somehow been the victims of a mugging – they were walking quietly down the corridor and suddenly somebody imposed a deadline on them. It seems to me that if I, as the project manager, accept something which you as management or customer pass to me – irrespective of how much pressure you put on me to accept it – it's not so much a mugging, it's more like a conspiracy to commit a felony. You thought up the crime and I agreed to go along with it. Who's at fault here? You, for thinking up the crime, or me, for accepting it?

Not all projects – as they are offered to you – are possible. You need to make very clear, up front and over the life of the project, what the project stakeholders – in particular, the customer and the management – can expect from the project. Chapters 6 and 7 are about how to do that.

> **"You need to make very clear, what the project stakeholders can expect from the project"**

10 The project was planned properly, but then progress against the plan was not monitored properly

The detailed chaining together of jobs is your chart through the shoals of the project. For you to develop the plan, only to throw it away or disregard it, particularly when pressure comes on, is lunacy for which you truly do deserve to suffer. Chapter 8 describes how to track the plan properly.

11 Project reporting was inadequate or non-existent

Most status reports are packed full of incident, but manage to conceal utterly any useful information, like whether the project is on target or not, or what the current big issues are. Lack of project reporting on its own isn't enough to sink the project, but it certainly doesn't help. Chapter 8 describes proper project reporting.

12 When the project got into trouble, people believed the problem could be solved by some simple action, e.g. work harder, extend the deadline, add more resources

In general, it can't. If the project gets into trouble it's because somebody got the planning wrong. If this happens to you, then what you need to do is to go back and plan it all over again as described in Chapters 1–7.

If the project gets into trouble it's because somebody got the planning wrong

APPENDIX

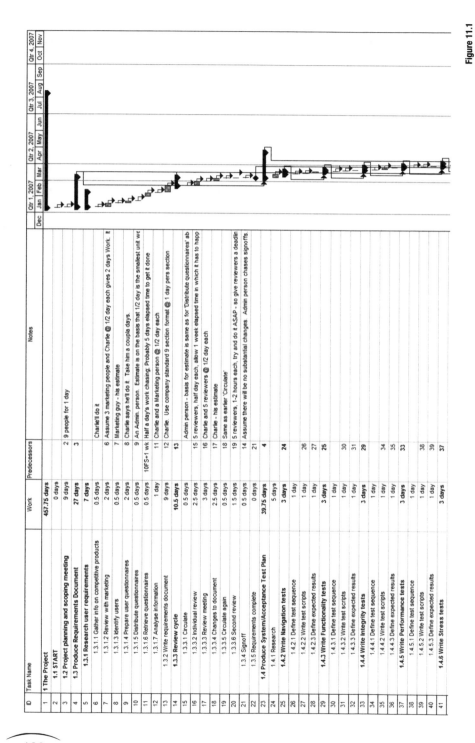

ID	Task Name	Work	Predecessors	Notes
1	**1 The Project**	**457.75 days**		
2	**1.1 START**	**0 days**		
3	**1.2 Project planning and scoping meeting**	**9 days**	2	9 people for 1 day
4	**1.3 Produce Requirements Document**	**27 days**	3	
5	**1.3.1 Research user requirements**	**7 days**		
6	1.3.1.1 Gather info on competitive products	0.5 days		Charlie'll do it
7	1.3.1.2 Review with marketing	2 days	6	Assume 3 marketing people and Charlie @ 1/2 day each gives 2 days Work. It
8	1.3.1.3 Identify users	0.5 days	7	Marketing guy - his estimate
9	1.3.1.4 Prepare user questionnaires	2 days	8	Charlie says he'll do it. Take him a coupla days.
10	1.3.1.5 Distribute questionnaires	0.5 days	9	An Admin. person. Estimate is on the basis that 1/2 day is the smallest unit we
11	1.3.1.6 Retrieve questionnaires	0.5 days	10FS+1 wk	Half a day's work chasing. Probably 5 days elapsed time to get it done
12	1.3.1.7 Analyse information	1 day	11	Charlie and a Marketing person @ 1/2 day each
13	1.3.2 Write requirements document	9 days	12	Charlie. Use company standard 9 section format @ 1 day pers section
14	**1.3.3 Review cycle**	**10.5 days**	13	
15	1.3.3.1 Circulate	0.5 days		Admin person - basis for estimate is same as for 'Distribute questionnaires' ab
16	1.3.3.2 Individual review	2.5 days	15	5 reviewers, half day each, allow 1 week elapsed time in which it has to happ
17	1.3.3.3 Review meeting	3 days	16	Charlie and 5 reviewers @ 1/2 day each
18	1.3.3.4 Changes to document	2.5 days	17	Charlie - his estimate
19	1.3.3.5 Circulate again	0.5 days	18	Same as earlier 'Circulate'
20	1.3.3.6 Second review	1.5 days	19	5 reviewers, 1-2 hours each, try and do it ASAP - so give reviewers a deadlin
21	1.3.4 Signoff	0.5 days	14	Assume there will be no substantial changes. Admin person chases signoffs.
22	1.3.5 Requirements complete	0 days	21	
23	**1.4 Produce System/Acceptance Test Plan**	**39.75 days**	4	
24	1.4.1 Research	5 days		
25	**1.4.2 Write Navigation tests**	**3 days**	24	
26	1.4.2.1 Define test sequence	1 day		
27	1.4.2.2 Write test scripts	1 day	26	
28	1.4.2.3 Define expected results	1 day	27	
29	**1.4.3 Write Functionality tests**	**3 days**	25	
30	1.4.3.1 Define test sequence	1 day		
31	1.4.3.2 Write test scripts	1 day	30	
32	1.4.3.3 Define expected results	1 day	31	
33	**1.4.4 Write Integrity tests**	**3 days**	29	
34	1.4.4.1 Define test sequence	1 day		
35	1.4.4.2 Write test scripts	1 day	34	
36	1.4.4.3 Define expected results	1 day	35	
37	**1.4.5 Write Performance tests**	**3 days**	33	
38	1.4.5.1 Define test sequence	1 day		
39	1.4.5.2 Write test scripts	1 day	38	
40	1.4.5.3 Define expected results	1 day	39	
41	**1.4.6 Write Stress tests**	**3 days**	37	

Figure 11.1

#	Task Name	Duration	ID	Notes
42	1.4.6.1 Define test sequence	1 day	42	
43	1.4.6.2 Write test scripts	1 day	42	
44	1.4.6.3 Define expected results	1 day	43	
45	**1.4.7 Write installation tests**	3 days	41	
46	1.4.7.1 Define test sequence	1 day	46	
47	1.4.7.2 Write test scripts	1 day	46	
48	1.4.7.3 Define expected results	1 day	47	
49	**1.4.8 Review cycle**	16.25 days	45	
50	1.4.8.1 Circulate	0.5 days	50	Assume 5 reviewers @ 1 day each
51	1.4.8.2 Individual review	5 days	51	
52	1.4.8.3 Review meeting	3.5 days	52	
53	1.4.8.4 Changes to document	5 days	53	
54	1.4.8.5 Circulate again	0.5 days	54	
55	1.4.8.6 Second review	1.75 days	54	
56	1.4.9 Signoff	0.5 days	49	
57	1.4.10 System/Acceptance tests written	0 days	56	
58	**1.5 Prototype**	22 days	4	Assuming people are available immediately) to review the work. So the 22 day
59	**1.6 Write code**	184 days	58	
60	**1.6.1 Pricing**	8 days		
61	1.6.1.1 Write code element (including clean cor	4 days		
62	1.6.1.2 Document code element:	0.5 days		
63	**1.6.1.3 Unit test code**	3.5 days	62	
64	**1.6.1.3.1 Prepare test Plan and test s**	1 day	62	
65	1.6.1.3.1.1 Define test sequence	0.25 days	65	
66	1.6.1.3.1.2 Write test scripts	0.5 days	66	
67	1.6.1.3.1.3 Define expected results	0.25 days	67	
68	1.6.1.3.2 Subsystem ready for unit testing	0 days	68	
69	1.6.1.3.3 Test code	1 day	69	
70	1.6.1.3.4 Make corrections to code	0.5 days	70	
71	1.6.1.3.5 Test code again	0.5 days	71	
72	1.6.1.3.6 Prepare test report	0.5 days		
73	**1.6.2 Settlement**	8 days		
74	1.6.2.1 Write code element (including clean cor	4 days		
75	1.6.2.2 Document code element	0.5 days		
76	**1.6.2.3 Unit test code**	3.5 days	75	
77	**1.6.2.3.1 Prepare test Plan and test s**	1 day	75	
78	1.6.2.3.1.1 Define test sequence	0.25 days	78	
79	1.6.2.3.1.2 Write test scripts	0.5 days	79	
80	1.6.2.3.1.3 Define expected results	0.25 days	80	
81	1.6.2.3.2 Subsystem ready for unit testing	0 days	80	
82	1.6.2.3.3 Test code	1 day	81	
83	1.6.2.3.4 Make corrections to code	0.5 days	82	
84	1.6.2.3.5 Test code again	0.5 days	83	

Figure 11.1 Continued

	Task	Duration	
85	1.6.2.3.6 Prepare test report	0.5 days	84
86	**1.6.3 Reporting**	**8 days**	
87	1.6.3.1 Write code element (including clean cor	4 days	
88	1.6.3.2 Document code element	0.5 days	
89	**1.6.3.3 Unit test code**	**3.5 days**	**88**
90	**1.6.3.3.1 Prepare test Plan and test sc**	**1 day**	
91	1.6.3.3.1.1 Define test sequence	0.25 days	91
92	1.6.3.3.1.2 Write test scripts	0.5 days	92
93	1.6.3.3.1.3 Define expected results	0.25 days	93
94	1.6.3.3.2 Subsystem ready for unit testing	0 days	94
95	1.6.3.3.3 Test code	1 day	95
96	1.6.3.3.4 Make corrections to code	0.5 days	96
97	1.6.3.3.5 Test code again	0.5 days	97
98	1.6.3.3.6 Prepare test report	0.5 days	
99	**1.6.4 Foreign exchange**	**16 days**	
100	1.6.4.1 Write code element (including clean cor	8 days	
101	1.6.4.2 Document code element	1 day	**101**
102	**1.6.4.3 Unit test code**	**7 days**	
103	**1.6.4.3.1 Prepare test Plan and test sc**	**2 days**	
104	1.6.4.3.1.1 Define test sequence	0.5 days	104
105	1.6.4.3.1.2 Write test scripts	1 day	105
106	1.6.4.3.1.3 Define expected results	0.5 days	
107	1.6.4.3.2 Subsystem ready for unit testing	0 days	106
108	1.6.4.3.3 Test code	2 days	107
109	1.6.4.3.4 Make corrections to code	1 day	108
110	1.6.4.3.5 Test code again	1 day	109
111	1.6.4.3.6 Prepare test report	1 day	110
112	**1.6.5 Euro support**	**16 days**	
113	1.6.5.1 Write code element (including clean cor	8 days	
114	1.6.5.2 Document code element	1 day	**114**
115	**1.6.5.3 Unit test code**	**7 days**	
116	**1.6.5.3.1 Prepare test Plan and test sc**	**2 days**	
117	1.6.5.3.1.1 Define test sequence	0.5 days	117
118	1.6.5.3.1.2 Write test scripts	1 day	118
119	1.6.5.3.1.3 Define expected results	0.5 days	119
120	1.6.5.3.2 Subsystem ready for unit testing	0 days	120
121	1.6.5.3.3 Test code	2 days	121
122	1.6.5.3.4 Make corrections to code	1 day	122
123	1.6.5.3.5 Test code again	1 day	123
124	1.6.5.3.6 Prepare test report	1 day	
125	**1.6.6 3rd party payments**	**16 days**	
126	1.6.6.1 Write code element (including clean cor	8 days	
127	1.6.6.2 Document code element	1 day	

Figure 11.1 Continued

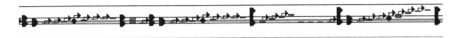

	Task Name	Duration	Pred
128	**1.6.6.3 Unit test code**	**7 days**	**127**
129	**1.6.6.3.1 Prepare test Plan and test se**	**2 days**	
130	1.6.6.3.1.1 Define test sequence	0.5 days	
131	1.6.6.3.1.2 Write test scripts	1 day	130
132	1.6.6.3.1.3 Define expected results	0.5 days	131
133	1.6.6.3.2 Subsystem ready for unit testing	2 days	132
134	1.6.6.3.3 Test code	1 day	133
135	1.6.6.3.4 Make corrections to code	1 day	134
136	1.6.6.3.5 Test code again	1 day	135
137	1.6.6.3.6 Prepare test report		136
138	**1.6.7 Tutorial**	**16 days**	
139	1.6.7.1 Write code element (including clean cor	8 days	
140	1.6.7.2 Document code element	1 day	
141	**1.6.7.3 Unit test code**	**7 days**	**140**
142	**1.6.7.3.1 Prepare test Plan and test se**	**2 days**	
143	1.6.7.3.1.1 Define test sequence	0.5 days	
144	1.6.7.3.1.2 Write test scripts	1 day	143
145	1.6.7.3.1.3 Define expected results	0.5 days	144
146	1.6.7.3.2 Subsystem ready for unit testing	0 days	145
147	1.6.7.3.3 Test code	2 days	146
148	1.6.7.3.4 Make corrections to code	1 day	147
149	1.6.7.3.5 Test code again	1 day	148
150	1.6.7.3.6 Prepare test report	1 day	149
151	**1.6.8 Web interface**	**32 days**	
152	1.6.8.1 Write code element 1 (including clean c	3 days	
153	1.6.8.2 Write code element 2 (including clean c	3 days	152
154	1.6.8.3 Write code element 3 (including clean c	3 days	153
155	1.6.8.4 Write code element 4 (including clean c	3 days	154
156	1.6.8.5 Document code element 1	1 day	
157	1.6.8.6 Document code element 2	1 day	
158	1.6.8.7 Document code element 3	1 day	
159	1.6.8.8 Document code element 4	1 day	
160	**1.6.8.9 Unit test code**	**16 days**	**159**
161	**1.6.8.9.1 Prepare test Plan and test se**	**4 days**	
162	1.6.8.9.1.1 Define test sequence	1 day	
163	1.6.8.9.1.2 Write test scripts	2 days	162
164	1.6.8.9.1.3 Define expected results	1 day	163
165	1.6.8.9.2 Subsystem ready for unit testing	6 days	164
166	1.6.8.9.3 Test code	2 days	165
167	1.6.8.9.4 Make corrections to code	2 days	166
168	1.6.8.9.5 Test code again	2 days	167
169	1.6.8.9.6 Prepare test report	2 days	168
170	**1.6.9 Security**	**32 days**	

Figure 11.1 Continued

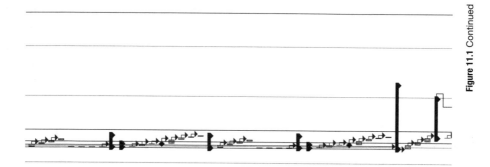

Figure 11.1 Continued

#	Task	Duration	
171	1.6.9.1 Write code element 1 (including clean c	3 days	
172	1.6.9.2 Write code element 2 (including clean c	3 days	171
173	1.6.9.3 Write code element 3 (including clean c	3 days	172
174	1.6.9.4 Write code element 4 (including clean c	3 days	173
175	1.6.9.5 Document code element 1	1 day	
176	1.6.9.6 Document code element 2	1 day	
177	1.6.9.7 Document code element 3	1 day	
178	1.6.9.8 Document code element 4	1 day	
179	**1.6.9.9 Unit test code**	**16 days**	**178**
180	**1.6.9.9.1 Prepare test Plan and test se**	**4 days**	
181	1.6.9.9.1.1 Define test sequence	1 day	
182	1.6.9.9.1.2 Write test scripts	2 days	181
183	1.6.9.9.1.3 Define expected results	1 day	182
184	1.6.9.9.2 Subsystem ready for unit testing	0 days	183
185	1.6.9.9.3 Test code	6 days	184
186	1.6.9.9.4 Make corrections to code	2 days	185
187	1.6.9.9.5 Test code again	2 days	186
188	1.6.9.9.6 Prepare test report	2 days	187
189	**1.6.10 Online help**	**32 days**	
190	1.6.10.1 Write code element 1 (including clean	3 days	
191	1.6.10.2 Write code element 2 (including clean	3 days	190
192	1.6.10.3 Write code element 3 (including clean	3 days	191
193	1.6.10.4 Write code element 4 (including clean	3 days	192
194	1.6.10.5 Document code element 1	1 day	
195	1.6.10.6 Document code element 2	1 day	
196	1.6.10.7 Document code element 3	1 day	
197	1.6.10.8 Document code element 4	1 day	
198	**1.6.10.9 Unit test code**	**16 days**	**197**
199	**1.6.10.9.1 Prepare test Plan and test s**	**4 days**	
200	1.6.10.9.1.1 Define test sequence	1 day	
201	1.6.10.9.1.2 Write test scripts	2 days	200
202	1.6.10.9.1.3 Define expected results	1 day	201
203	1.6.10.9.2 Subsystem ready for unit testin	0 days	202
204	1.6.10.9.3 Test code	6 days	203
205	1.6.10.9.4 Make corrections to code	2 days	204
206	1.6.10.9.5 Test code again	2 days	205
207	1.6.10.9.6 Prepare test report	2 days	206
208	**1.7 Produce User Documentation and Help system**	**99 days**	**58**
209	1.7.1 Research requirements	5 days	22
210	1.7.2 Set up environment and tools	5 days	209
211	1.7.3 Define style sheet and produce prototype	5 days	210
212	**1.7.4 Write user documentation or Help text**	**53 days**	**211**
213	1.7.4.1 Structure into chapters	1 day	

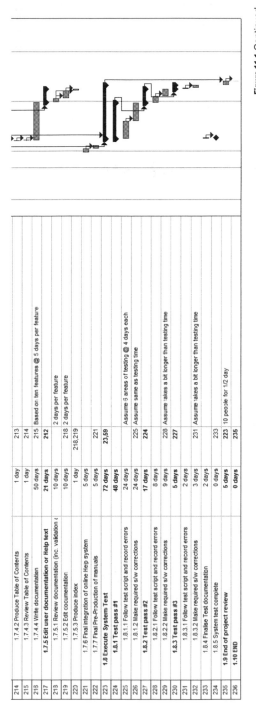

	Task Name	Duration		Notes
214	1.7.4.2 Produce Table of Contents	1 day	213	
215	1.7.4.3 Review Table of Contents	1 day	214	
216	1.7.4.4 Write documentation	50 days	215	Based on ten features @ 5 days per feature
217	**1.7.5 Edit user documentation or Help text**	**21 days**	**212**	
218	1.7.5.1 Review documentation (inc. validation &	10 days		2 days per feature
219	1.7.5.2 Edit documentation	10 days	218	2 days per feature
220	1.7.5.3 Produce index	1 day	218,219	
221	1.7.6 Final integration of online Help system	5 days		
222	1.7.7 Final Pre-Production of manuals	5 days	221	
223	**1.8 Execute System Test**	**72 days**	**23,59**	
224	**1.8.1 Test pass #1**	**48 days**		
225	1.8.1.1 Follow test script and record errors	24 days		Assume 3 areas of testing @ 4 days each
226	1.8.1.2 Make required s/w corrections	24 days	225	Assume same as testing time
227	**1.8.2 Test pass #2**	**17 days**	**224**	
228	1.8.2.1 Follow test script and record errors	8 days		Assume takes a bit longer than testing time
229	1.8.2.2 Make required s/w corrections	9 days	228	
230	**1.8.3 Test pass #3**	**5 days**	**227**	
231	1.8.3.1 Follow test script and record errors	2 days		Assume takes a bit longer than testing time
232	1.8.3.2 Make required s/w corrections	3 days	231	
233	1.8.4 Finalise Test documentation	2 days		
234	1.8.5 System test complete	0 days	233	
235	**1.9 End of project review**	**5 days**	**223**	10 people for 1/2 day
236	**1.10 END**	**0 days**	**235**	

Figure 11.1 Continued

ID	Task Name	Work	Predecessor	Resource Names	Duration
1	**1 The Project**	**610 days**			**154 days**
2	**1.1 START**	0 days			0 days
3	**1.2 Project planning and scoping meeting**	9 days	2		1 day
4	**1.3 Produce Requirements Document**	**27 days**	3		**39.5 days**
5	**1.3.1 Research user requirements**	**7 days**			**19.5 days**
6	1.3.1.1 Gather info on competitive products	0.5 days		Charlie	0.5 days
7	1.3.1.2 Review with marketing	2 days	6	Analyst #1[20%	5 days
8	1.3.1.3 Identify users	0.5 days	7	Marketing guy	0.5 days
9	1.3.1.4 Prepare user questionnaires	2 days	8	Charlie	2 days
10	1.3.1.5 Distribute questionnaires	0.5 days	9	Administrative A	0.5 days
11	1.3.1.6 Retrieve questionnaires	0.5 days	10FS+1 wk	Administrative A	5 days
12	1.3.1.7 Analyse information	1 day	11	Analysts	1 day
13	1.3.2 Write requirements document	9 days	12	Charlie	9 days
14	**1.3.3 Review cycle**	**10.5 days**	13		**10.5 days**
15	1.3.3.1 Circulate	0.5 days		Administrative A	0.5 days
16	1.3.3.2 Individual review	2.5 days	15	Requirements R	5 days
17	1.3.3.3 Review meeting	3 days	16		0.5 days
18	1.3.3.4 Changes to document	2.5 days	17	Charlie	2.5 days
19	1.3.3.5 Circulate again	0.5 days	18	Administrative A	0.5 days
20	1.3.3.6 Second review	1.5 days	19		0.5 days
21	1.3.4 Signoff	0.5 days	14	Administrative A	0.5 days
22	1.3.5 Requirements complete	0 days	21		0 days
23	**1.4 Produce System/Acceptance Test Plan**	**40 days**	4		**33 days**
24	1.4.1 Research	5 days		Tester #1	5 days
25	**1.4.2 Write Navigation tests**	**3 days**	24		**3 days**
26	1.4.2.1 Define test sequence	1 day		Tester #1	1 day
27	1.4.2.2 Write test scripts	1 day	26	Tester #1	1 day
28	1.4.2.3 Define expected results	1 day	27	Tester #1	1 day
29	**1.4.3 Write Functionality tests**	**3 days**	25		**3 days**
30	1.4.3.1 Define test sequence	1 day		Tester #1	1 day
31	1.4.3.2 Write test scripts	1 day	30	Tester #1	1 day

Figure 11.2

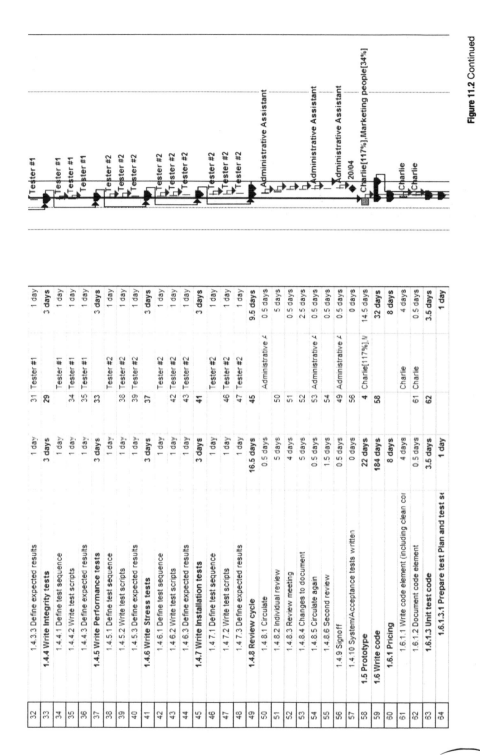

Figure 11.2 Continued

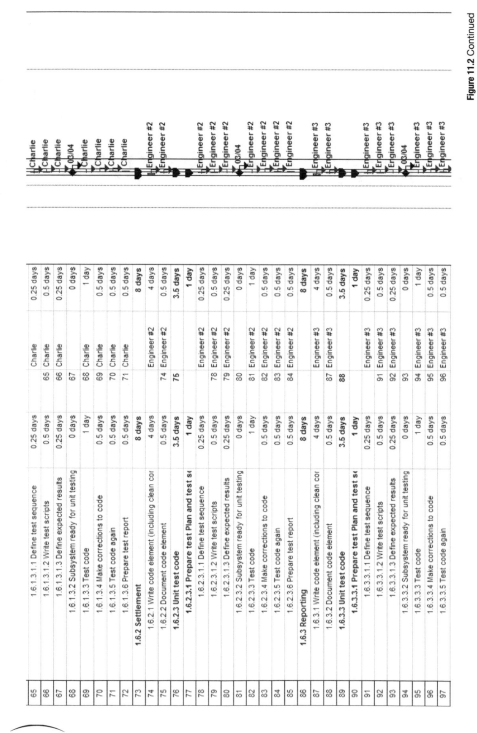

ID	Task Name	Duration	Resource Names
65	1.6.1.3.1.1 Define test sequence	0.25 days	Charlie
66	1.6.1.3.1.2 Write test scripts	0.5 days	Charlie
67	1.6.1.3.1.3 Define expected results	0.25 days	Charlie
68	1.6.1.3.2 Subsystem ready for unit testing	0 days	Charlie 03/04
69	1.6.1.3.3 Test code	1 day	Charlie
70	1.6.1.3.4 Make corrections to code	0.5 days	Charlie
71	1.6.1.3.5 Test code again	0.5 days	Charlie
72	1.6.1.3.6 Prepare test report	0.5 days	Charlie
73	**1.6.2 Settlement**	**8 days**	
74	1.6.2.1 Write code element (including clean cor	4 days	Engineer #2
75	1.6.2.2 Document code element	0.5 days	Engineer #2
76	**1.6.2.3 Unit test code**	**3.5 days**	
77	**1.6.2.3.1 Prepare test Plan and test se**	**1 day**	
78	1.6.2.3.1.1 Define test sequence	0.25 days	Engineer #2
79	1.6.2.3.1.2 Write test scripts	0.5 days	Engineer #2
80	1.6.2.3.1.3 Define expected results	0.25 days	Engineer #2
81	1.6.2.3.2 Subsystem ready for unit testing	0 days	Engineer #2 03/04
82	1.6.2.3.3 Test code	1 day	Engineer #2
83	1.6.2.3.4 Make corrections to code	0.5 days	Engineer #2
84	1.6.2.3.5 Test code again	0.5 days	Engineer #2
85	1.6.2.3.6 Prepare test report	0.5 days	Engineer #2
86	**1.6.3 Reporting**	**8 days**	
87	1.6.3.1 Write code element (including clean cor	4 days	Engineer #3
88	1.6.3.2 Document code element	0.5 days	Engineer #3
89	**1.6.3.3 Unit test code**	**3.5 days**	
90	**1.6.3.3.1 Prepare test Plan and test se**	**1 day**	
91	1.6.3.3.1.1 Define test sequence	0.25 days	Engineer #3
92	1.6.3.3.1.2 Write test scripts	0.5 days	Engineer #3
93	1.6.3.3.1.3 Define expected results	0.25 days	Engineer #3
94	1.6.3.3.2 Subsystem ready for unit testing	0 days	Engineer #3 03/04
95	1.6.3.3.3 Test code	1 day	Engineer #3
96	1.6.3.3.4 Make corrections to code	0.5 days	Engineer #3
97	1.6.3.3.5 Test code again	0.5 days	Engineer #3

Figure 11.2 Continued

ID	Task Name	Duration	Resource
98	1.6.3.3.6 Prepare test report	0.5 days	Engineer #3
99	**1.6.4 Foreign exchange**	**16 days**	
100	1.6.4.1 Write code element (including clean cor	8 days	Engineer #4
101	1.6.4.2 Document code element	1 day	Engineer #4
102	**1.6.4.3 Unit test code**	**7 days**	
103	**1.6.4.3.1 Prepare test Plan and test se**	**2 days**	
104	1.6.4.3.1.1 Define test sequence	0.5 days	Engineer #4
105	1.6.4.3.1.2 Write test scripts	1 day	Engineer #4
106	1.6.4.3.1.3 Define expected results	0.5 days	Engineer #4
107	1.6.4.3.2 Subsystem ready for unit testing	0 days	
108	1.6.4.3.3 Test code	2 days	Engineer #4
109	1.6.4.3.4 Make corrections to code	1 day	Engineer #4
110	1.6.4.3.5 Test code again	1 day	Engineer #4
111	1.6.4.3.6 Prepare test report	1 day	Engineer #4
112	**1.6.5 Euro support**	**16 days**	
113	1.6.5.1 Write code element (including clean cor	8 days	Engineer #4
114	1.6.5.2 Document code element	1 day	Engineer #4
115	**1.6.5.3 Unit test code**	**7 days**	
116	**1.6.5.3.1 Prepare test Plan and test se**	**2 days**	
117	1.6.5.3.1.1 Define test sequence	0.5 days	Engineer #4
118	1.6.5.3.1.2 Write test scripts	1 day	Engineer #4
119	1.6.5.3.1.3 Define expected results	0.5 days	Engineer #4
120	1.6.5.3.2 Subsystem ready for unit testing	0 days	
121	1.6.5.3.3 Test code	2 days	Engineer #4
122	1.6.5.3.4 Make corrections to code	1 day	Engineer #4
123	1.6.5.3.5 Test code again	1 day	Engineer #4
124	1.6.5.3.6 Prepare test report	1 day	Engineer #4
125	**1.6.6 3rd party payments**	**16 days**	
126	1.6.6.1 Write code element (including clean cor	8 days	Engineer #4
127	1.6.6.2 Document code element	1 day	Engineer #4
128	**1.6.6.3 Unit test code**	**7 days**	
129	**1.6.6.3.1 Prepare test Plan and test se**	**2 days**	
130	1.6.6.3.1.1 Define test sequence	0.5 days	Engineer #4

Figure 11.2 Continued

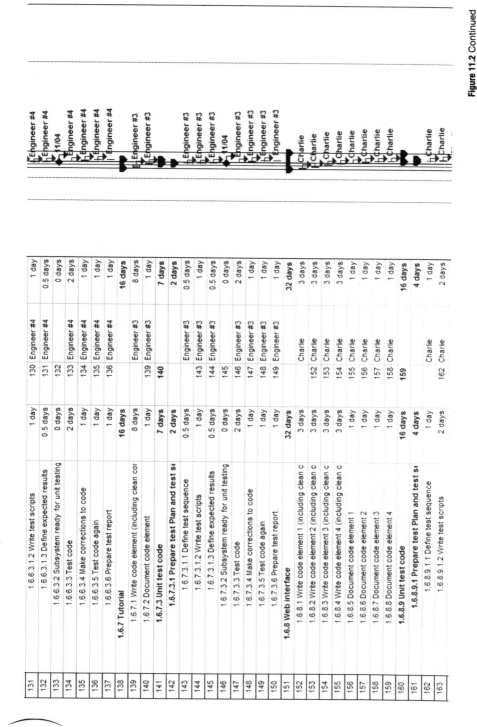

ID	Task name	Duration	ID	Resource	Duration
131	1.6.6.3.1.2 Write test scripts	1 day	130	Engineer #4	1 day
132	1.6.6.3.1.1.3 Define expected results	0.5 days	131	Engineer #4	0.5 days
133	1.6.6.3.2 Subsystem ready for unit testing	0 days	132		0 days
134	1.6.6.3.3 Test code	2 days	133	Engineer #4	2 days
135	1.6.6.3.4 Make corrections to code	1 day	134	Engineer #4	1 day
136	1.6.6.3.5 Test code again	1 day	135	Engineer #4	1 day
137	1.6.6.3.6 Prepare test report	1 day	136	Engineer #4	1 day
138	**1.6.7 Tutorial**	**16 days**			**16 days**
139	1.6.7.1 Write code element (including clean cor	8 days	139	Engineer #3	8 days
140	1.6.7.2 Document code element	1 day	140	Engineer #3	1 day
141	**1.6.7.3 Unit test code**	**7 days**	**140**		**7 days**
142	**1.6.7.3.1 Prepare test Plan and test se**	**2 days**			**2 days**
143	1.6.7.3.1.1 Define test sequence	0.5 days	143	Engineer #3	0.5 days
144	1.6.7.3.1.2 Write test scripts	1 day	144	Engineer #3	1 day
145	1.6.7.3.1.3 Define expected results	0.5 days	145	Engineer #3	0.5 days
146	1.6.7.3.2 Subsystem ready for unit testing	0 days	145		0 days
147	1.6.7.3.3 Test code	2 days	146	Engineer #3	2 days
148	1.6.7.3.4 Make corrections to code	1 day	147	Engineer #3	1 day
149	1.6.7.3.5 Test code again	1 day	148	Engineer #3	1 day
150	1.6.7.3.6 Prepare test report	1 day	149	Engineer #3	1 day
151	**1.6.8 Web interface**	**32 days**			**32 days**
152	1.6.8.1 Write code element 1 (including clean c	3 days	152	Charlie	3 days
153	1.6.8.2 Write code element 2 (including clean c	3 days	153	Charlie	3 days
154	1.6.8.3 Write code element 3 (including clean c	3 days	154	Charlie	3 days
155	1.6.8.4 Write code element 4 (including clean c	3 days	155	Charlie	3 days
156	1.6.8.5 Document code element 1	1 day	156	Charlie	1 day
157	1.6.8.6 Document code element 2	1 day	157	Charlie	1 day
158	1.6.8.7 Document code element 3	1 day	158	Charlie	1 day
159	1.6.8.8 Document code element 4	1 day	159	Charlie	1 day
160	**1.6.8.9 Unit test code**	**16 days**	**159**		**16 days**
161	**1.6.8.9.1 Prepare test Plan and test se**	**4 days**			**4 days**
162	1.6.8.9.1.1 Define test sequence	1 day	162	Charlie	1 day
163	1.6.8.9.1.2 Write test scripts	2 days		Charlie	2 days

Figure 11.2 Continued

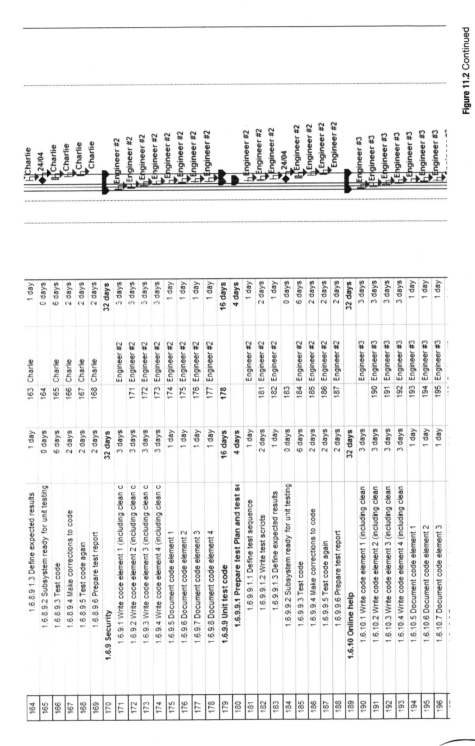

Figure 11.2 Continued

	Task Name	Duration	ID	Resource
164	1.6.8.9.1.3 Define expected results	1 day	163	Charlie
165	1.6.8.9.2 Subsystem ready for unit testing	0 days	164	
166	1.6.8.9.3 Test code	6 days	165	Charlie
167	1.6.8.9.4 Make corrections to code	2 days	166	Charlie
168	1.6.8.9.5 Test code again	2 days	167	Charlie
169	1.6.8.9.6 Prepare test report	2 days	168	Charlie
170	**1.6.9 Security**	**32 days**		
171	1.6.9.1 Write code element 1 (including clean c	3 days		Engineer #2
172	1.6.9.2 Write code element 2 (including clean c	3 days	171	Engineer #2
173	1.6.9.3 Write code element 3 (including clean c	3 days	172	Engineer #2
174	1.6.9.4 Write code element 4 (including clean c	3 days	173	Engineer #2
175	1.6.9.5 Document code element 1	1 day	174	Engineer #2
176	1.6.9.6 Document code element 2	1 day	175	Engineer #2
177	1.6.9.7 Document code element 3	1 day	176	Engineer #2
178	1.6.9.8 Document code element 4	1 day	177	Engineer #2
179	**1.6.9.9 Unit test code**	**16 days**	178	
180	**1.6.9.9.1 Prepare test Plan and test se**	**4 days**		
181	1.6.9.9.1.1 Define test sequence	1 day		Engineer #2
182	1.6.9.9.1.2 Write test scripts	2 days	181	Engineer #2
183	1.6.9.9.1.3 Define expected results	1 day	182	Engineer #2
184	1.6.9.9.2 Subsystem ready for unit testing	0 days	183	
185	1.6.9.3 Test code	6 days	184	Engineer #2
186	1.6.9.9.4 Make corrections to code	2 days	185	Engineer #2
187	1.6.9.5 Test code again	2 days	186	Engineer #2
188	1.6.9.9.6 Prepare test report	2 days	187	Engineer #2
189	**1.6.10 Online help**	**32 days**		
190	1.6.10.1 Write code element 1 (including clean	3 days		Engineer #3
191	1.6.10.2 Write code element 2 (including clean	3 days	190	Engineer #3
192	1.6.10.3 Write code element 3 (including clean	3 days	191	Engineer #3
193	1.6.10.4 Write code element 4 (including clean	3 days	192	Engineer #3
194	1.6.10.5 Document code element 1	1 day	193	Engineer #3
195	1.6.10.6 Document code element 2	1 day	194	Engineer #3
196	1.6.10.7 Document code element 3	1 day	195	Engineer #3

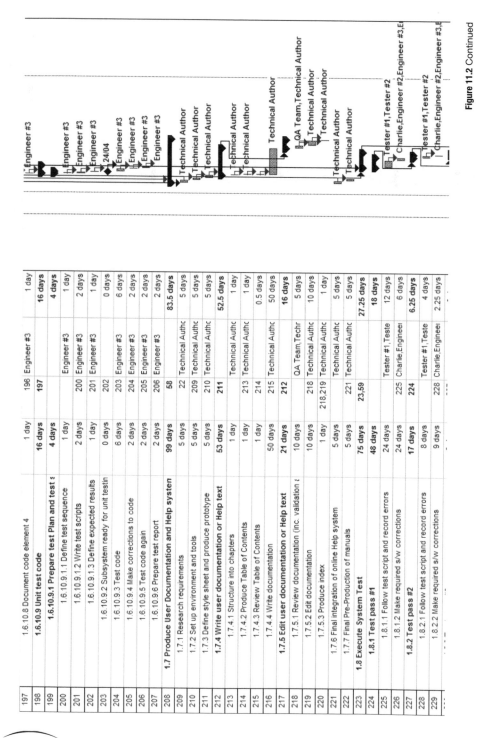

Figure 11.2 Continued

ID	Task Name	Duration	Pred	Resource	Duration	Resource Names
197	1.6.10.8 Document code element 4	1 day	196	Engineer #3	1 day	Engineer #3
198	**1.6.10.9 Unit test code**	16 days	197		16 days	
199	**1.6.10.9.1 Prepare test Plan and test s**	4 days			4 days	
200	1.6.10.9.1.1 Define test sequence	1 day		Engineer #3	1 day	Engineer #3
201	1.6.10.9.1.2 Write test scripts	2 days	200	Engineer #3	2 days	Engineer #3
202	1.6.10.9.1.3 Define expected results	1 day	201	Engineer #3	1 day	Engineer #3
203	1.6.10.9.2 Subsystem ready for unit testin	0 days	202		0 days	
204	1.6.10.9.3 Test code	6 days	203	Engineer #3	6 days	Engineer #3
205	1.6.10.9.4 Make corrections to code	2 days	204	Engineer #3	2 days	Engineer #3
206	1.6.10.9.5 Test code again	2 days	205	Engineer #3	2 days	Engineer #3
207	1.6.10.9.6 Prepare test report	2 days	206	Engineer #3	2 days	Engineer #3
208	**1.7 Produce User Documentation and Help system**	99 days	58		83.5 days	
209	1.7.1 Research requirements	5 days	22	Technical Auth	5 days	Technical Author
210	1.7.2 Set up environment and tools	5 days	209	Technical Auth	5 days	Technical Author
211	1.7.3 Define style sheet and produce prototype	5 days	210	Technical Auth	5 days	Technical Author
212	**1.7.4 Write user documentation or Help text**	53 days	211		52.5 days	
213	1.7.4.1 Structure into chapters	1 day		Technical Auth	1 day	Technical Author
214	1.7.4.2 Produce Table of Contents	1 day	213	Technical Auth	1 day	Technical Author
215	1.7.4.3 Review Table of Contents	1 day	214		0.5 days	Technical Author
216	1.7.4.4 Write documentation	50 days	215	Technical Auth	50 days	Technical Author
217	**1.7.5 Edit user documentation or Help text**	21 days	212		16 days	
218	1.7.5.1 Review documentation (inc. validation a	10 days		QA Team,Techn	5 days	QA Team,Technical Author
219	1.7.5.2 Edit documentation	10 days	218	Technical Auth	10 days	Technical Author
220	1.7.5.3 Produce index	1 day	218,219	Technical Auth	1 day	Technical Author
221	1.7.6 Final integration of online Help system	5 days		Technical Auth	5 days	Technical Author
222	1.7.7 Final Pre-Production of manuals	5 days	221	Technical Auth	5 days	Technical Author
223	**1.8 Execute System Test**	75 days	23,59		27.25 days	
224	**1.8.1 Test pass #1**	48 days			18 days	
225	1.8.1.1 Follow test script and record errors	24 days		Tester #1,Teste	12 days	Tester #1,Tester #2
226	1.8.1.2 Make required s/w corrections	24 days	225	Charlie,Enginee	6 days	Charlie,Engineer #2,Engineer #3,E
227	**1.8.2 Test pass #2**	17 days	224		6.25 days	
228	1.8.2.1 Follow test script and record errors	8 days		Tester #1,Teste	4 days	Tester #1,Tester #2
229	1.8.2.2 Make required s/w corrections	9 days	228	Charlie,Enginee	2.25 days	Charlie,Engineer #2,Engineer #3,E

230	**1.8.3 Test pass #3**	**8 days**	**227**		**3 days**
231	1.8.3.1 Follow test script and record errors	4 days		Tester #1,Teste	2 days
232	1.8.3.2 Make required s/w corrections	4 days	231	Charlie,Engineer	1 day
233	1.8.4 Finalise Test documentation	2 days		Tester #1,Teste	1 day
234	1.8.5 System test complete	0 days	233		0 days
235	**1.9 End of project review**	**5 days**	**223**	Team Members	5 days
236	**1.10 Project management**	**46 days**		You[33%]	140 days
237	**1.11 Contingency**	103 days	236	Team[7.36%]	14 days
238	**1.1 END**	**0 days**	235,237		0 days

Figure 11.2 Continued

BIBLIOGRAPHY

1 DeMarco, T. (1997) *The Deadline,* Dorset House Publishing.

2 Brooks, F.P. (1995) *The Mythical Man-Month,* Addison Wesley Longman.

INDEX

Page numbers in *italics* denotes figure

READ ON ...

BRILLIANT MANAGER
What the best managers *know, do and say*
Nic Peeling
▶ £12.99 ▶ 0-273-70213-0 ▶ 978-0-273-70213-9

Everything you've ever wanted to know about management – but were afraid to ask. This book is a refreshingly honest and practical guide to the best managerial practice, offering a handful of the most valuable things you need to know and do in a broad range of managerial situations. Read it, refer to it frequently and refresh your memory regularly. That way you'll be primed and prepared for every situation and will be on the managerial fast track for effectiveness and success.

You'll wonder how you ever managed without it...

FIVE STAR SERVICE ONE STAR BUDGET
How to create magic moments for your customers that get you noticed, remembered and referred
Michael Heppell
▶ £9.99 ▶ 0-273-70792-2 ▶ 978-0-273-70792-9

This book is the surest way to a more successful career for you and greater success for your organization. Bestselling author Michael Heppell shows you how the best customer service experience costs little if anything at all, but will win and retain you customers time after time, getting you noticed, remembered and referred. With over 100 instant tips, 50 examples of best practice, and multiple techniques and strategies, this book will equip you with a winning edge to impress your customers, deliver remarkable results, and fast track your career.

HOW TO LEAD
What you actually need to DO to manage, lead and succeed
Jo Owen
▶ £12.99 ▶ 0-273-69364-6 ▶ 978-0-273-69364-2

Whatever your level in an organization, this indispensable and entertaining guide to the core skills of leadership is the practical handbook for getting to the top and staying there. With authoritative guidance and stimulating and entertaining advice, this guide tells you what you actually need to DO to manage, lead and ultimately succeed.

ou can buy these books in all good bookshops,
r online at **www.pearson-books.com**

PEARSON
Prentice Hall
BUSINESS